MACHINE-QUILTED
JACKETS
VESTS
AND
COATS

MACHINE-QUILTED

JACKETS
VESTS
AND
COATS

CONTEMPORARY QUILTING

NANCY MOORE

Chilton Book Company

Radnor, Pennsylvania

Designed by Anthony Jacobson
Manufactured in the United States of America

Library of Congress Cataloging in Publication Data
Moore, Nancy (Nancy Lobmiller)
    Machine-quilted jackets, vests, and coats / Nancy Moore.
        p.   cm.—(Contemporary quilting series)
    Includes bibliographical references and index.
    ISBN 0-8019-8182-4 (hc)—ISBN 0-8019-8117-4 (pb)
    1. Coats.   2. Vests.   3. Machine quilting.   I. Title.
II. Series.
TT595.M66   1991
646.4′5—dc20   90-55880
                                              CIP

2 3 4 5 6 7 8 9 0   9 8 7 6 5 4 3 2

The following are registered trademark products mentioned in this book:

Adjust-A-Dart	Procion Dyes
Easy Way Pressing Sheet	Stacy Pattern Tracer
Fasturn	Stitch Witchery
Fray Check	Tear-A-Way
Hera Markers	Teflon Pressing Sheets
No More Pins	Unique Markers
Perfect Pleater	Unique Stitch
Press-On Fleece	Wonder Under

■ ■ ■
Contents

■
■

■ CONTENTS

Foreword

My favorite kind of writer has years of experience in three areas:

1. She has made lots of whatever she's writing about for her own pleasure. That implies she's conquered hundreds of the mistakes I will undoubtedly make.

2. She has tried to sell what she makes. Customers can reveal in seconds the flaws in design and construction of garments that took hours to sew.

3. She has taught others successfully. For a writer, this is particularly important. The class material must be structured in an organized, logical way. Questions must be anticipated and answered. Nothing can remain murky. And most importantly, she must convey her enthusiasm for the subject.

Nancy Moore is my kind of writer. She tells me to cut the lining 2″ longer because on the first jacket she made, the process of machine quilting caused the jacket lining to creep up. She knows that while customers want to buy a quilted jacket, they don't want to look like walking Japanese armor. And best of all, she inspired me to run for my beloved machine, where I'm using her unique technique (see Chapter 6) to dense-quilt a silk vest.

I hope Nancy will soon be one of your favorite writers, too.

Robbie Fanning

Robbie Fanning,
Series editor and co-author,
The Complete Book of Machine Quilting

■ ■ ■
Preface

Years of trial and error are represented in these pages. I always have sewn, but I began in earnest twelve years ago after retiring from my position as nutritionist for the county. My experience as a nutritionist was rewarding in the long-term sense, as I knew that I was providing balanced diets to create healthier individuals. But I came to the point in my life where I wanted to see my work rewarded more immediately and my projects finished more frequently.

Art classes, workshops in sewing techniques, and a class in dyeing at Arrowmont (an arts and crafts school in Gaithersburg, Tennessee) all seemed to lead to sewing. Designing one-of-a-kind clothing that looks good and is wearable for years was and is my goal. I make some quilts and wall hangings, but I always long to see an idea expressed in clothing. During the past twelve years, I have taught classes and sold garments at craft shows in the East and have met fine people who helped me develop my vision.

I have learned more with each completed project, and I want to share that knowledge with you in this book. I hope you find the same satisfaction I feel when I express myself through the clothing medium. I'll try to help you all I can. As one student in the last class I taught said, "Nancy, you never say anything is wrong; you just find a way to make it right." I wish I could be sitting by your shoulder to assist you as you experiment with the ideas found here.

The book never would have been written if I had not broken my foot a year-and-a-half ago. During this enforced quiet time, I reworked my lesson plans and came up with new ideas. I was able to sew with my left foot on the foot pedal and my right knee against the presser foot bar. Writing has given me a new challenge: learning to use a word processor. I hope the new accomplishments will never stop! Come with me on this adventure.

Nancy Lobmiller Moore
Wake Forest, North Carolina

Acknowledgments

Dedicated to my wonderful, patient family; and especially my mother, Mary McFarland Lobmiller, who started me on my sewing path.

Thanks to Ruth Steinberger and her assistant, Jan Taylor, for the drawings; Lee Phillips for the photographs; Glenda George, Elizabeth Chalk, Wendy Forte, Norma Smith, Kim Mack-Parker, and Brenda Spencer for sewing assistance; Marianne Beeson, Linda Ward, Susan Brittingham, and Lillie DeHart for technical assistance.

Thanks also to Marie Wood, Kathy Pierce, Elizabeth Chalk, and Barbara Wollan for the loan of garments they made; and to June Preston and Gary DuPree for computer help.

I also thank the following people and companies for the use of their materials: *Quilter's Newsletter Magazine,* Marilyn Stothers, Margaret Dittman, Yvonne Porcella, *Sew News,* Donna Poster, *American Quilter,* Clotilda, The Perfect Notion, Lois Ericson, Koss Van den Akken, Caryl Bryer Fallert, Joan Padgett, and The Crowning Touch, Inc.

A very special thank-you to all my customers and students over the years.

MACHINE-QUILTED
JACKETS
VESTS
AND
COATS

Introduction

The sewing machine is a wonderful tool that allows you to express your creative self. Since the sewing machine is primarily thought of as a woman's tool or machine, *let's use it* for the creation of art. Women have found many tools for creation in their homes—from the spoon to make a delicious cake to the rake to improve the landscape. Fancy equipment is not necessary for the ideas in this book. I originally developed the dense stitching on a thirty-five-year-old Singer.

I will describe how to make quilted outer garments that are uniquely yours. The chapter may say "jacket," but vests, coats, and capes can be made with the same instructions. When I say "uniquely yours," I hope to help you find your own style and infuse your own personality in the designs so that others can visually identify your work. Developing your own style takes practice, time, and creative desire. It means trying different crafts until you find what really feels good to you. Then work with the method enough to make it individual. To start the process and learn a new skill, it is necessary to copy ideas and patterns. As you progress you will leave copying behind and do the creative work yourself. It may turn out that you try everything in this book and none of the ideas feel like you, so you go back to basketmaking or whatever.

Basic sewing techniques and tools needed for the book are reviewed in the first chapter. If you are an inexperienced sewer, go over the techniques and use the resources listed to learn more skills.

The jacket in Chapter 2 (made with one fabric) is the easiest. You will get an idea of how to handle the fabric with batting and how to machine-quilt the jacket. Your first project will be finished in about nine hours.

Part II of this book has an example of piecing in depth and then presents other ways to embellish a jacket through piecing. It's hard to predict the amount of time you will spend because it depends on the method you use. Count on spending at least fifteen hours on each project. You may only be interested in trying a few of the ideas, or you may be teaching and want to work out samples of all the methods.

The newest of the techniques—the densely quilted jacket—is explained in Chapter 6. Early in the chapter I explain how I think the technique developed. It's a great look, very wearable, and it gets you admiring glances wherever you go. Dense quilting is not hard, but like many things it takes practice. If you have done fabric embroidery, Battenberg lace, or other techniques with the feed dogs down, you are steps ahead. The other thing that is different is the lack of precision in the method. No, we do not draw every line; no, the stitches are not always the same size—and it makes no difference. The process is not messy, but it does have a relaxed drawing component to it.

The methods for the ideas in the book are not new. I will try to give credit to the sewers who created the ideas when I know them. I always am distressed to see an idea presented by a writer or teacher as her own when I know someone else published it first. I read a great deal, and a red flag goes up when I read directions and say, "Ah, here's a new idea," or, "Oh, that's not new—it's an antique way to do that." Many ideas have been circulated, revamped, and revised through time, but I always will try to give credit where it is due.

It would be helpful to scan the book to find what interests you the most. In that way you will know where your experience will allow you to begin. Jackets in Chapters 3 and 4 are finished in the same way. The dense jackets in Chapter 6 have

another finish. All garments feature polyester-bonded batting unless otherwise noted. I am assuming that you know basic clothing construction and the operation of the sewing machine. No fancy machine is necessary to construct any of the jackets or sew any of the techniques. A knowledge of tailoring is not necessary. The skill level for the jackets is similar to making a blouse—a bulky blouse at that. Throughout the book I indicate where the serger can be used and any labor-saving techniques I have found.

The last chapter gives you some directions for designing for yourself and lists resources for more design information. I have found the greatest joy in creating my own designs and will encourage you to do the same. There is no such thing as not being able to design and draw for yourself if you have the desire. Slavish copying of other designs looks like what it is, but your own touch and spark make an item exciting to others and deeply satisfying to you. Why do we slave over these projects if, in the end, the satisfactions do not outweigh the labor? We certainly do not become rich doing it; at least I couldn't earn my living selling garments. However, you can supplement your income nicely while you enjoy creating. I will share with you some of my experiences in marketing my products.

I also present a few smaller projects and instructions: fun boots; three ways to use my ideas on skirts; adding a bust dart; an easy vest lining; adapting the machine quilting to quilts; and what I call "doodles," a scrap project.

Clean and oil your machine, buy the supplies for the first jacket, and let's get started.

PART I

GETTING STARTED

CHAPTER 1

■ ■ ■

Basic Sewing Techniques for Machine Quilting

Thank goodness, even if you have no background in sewing, it's never too late to learn more skills. Be patient with yourself and learn step by step.

In this first section we will detail your work space, equipment, and the skills needed to make a machine-quilted garment. More sewing information is available in the text. If you are unsure of a procedure, find an alternate reference in the index, or, if you don't understand my explanation, try some of the resources listed in the Bibliography. At least one basic sewing book is a must for every sewer. There *is* help.

■ Tools of the Trade

Work space is not an actual tool, but a well-arranged space certainly makes the job easier. You will not accomplish much if your space is not permanently set up so that you can work when you have bits of time. I've gone from having my machine on a table in a closet to an enclosed 11′ × 9′ sunporch that I grandly call my studio. (We all do better work with positive thinking.) In this small space I now have my machine, serger, computer, work table (made from a flush door), four-drawer file cabinet, and storage for notions and one-half of my fabric collection. The best features of the room are the windows on two sides. I can lean on the work table, watch the birds, watch the garden grow, and get my best ideas. Other designers' creative work spaces are shown in *Sew, Serge, Press* (noted in the Bibliography).

Necessary tools include:

A *sewing machine* that will meet the needs of your volume of work and skill in sewing is your first priority. Today straight and zigzag

Jacobean-style linen design usually done in crewel embroidery. I call this design "stylized flowers."

stitches are the minimum stitches needed. If you are new to sewing and not sure of your continued interest, see your local reputable dealer and get a used machine that won't cost as much as a new, top-of-the-line machine. It is vital to patronize a good local sewing machine dealer for repairs, training, and updates on your machine. A less-expensive mail-order machine is not a good deal in the long run. Read, test, and ask experienced sewers before making a decision. *Sew News* (listed in the Bibliography) presents a different machine each month, and *Threads* magazine has been running regular evaluations of both high- and low-end machines.

Once you have your machine, take a few hours to get acquainted with it. Read your instruction book and try all the ideas it contains. Take classes offered by your dealer. For machine quilting you will need to know how to lower the feed dogs, use the blind hemmer, and use the quilt guide. A darning (embroidery) foot is a must, as is a flat-bed extension if your machine is not set in a cabinet. An even-feed foot is great to have, but you can do without it.

Buy extra bobbins for your machine and good-quality needles recommended by your machine instruction book (e.g., Schmetz). Change your machine needle with every garment you make or earlier if the needle snags or the thread keeps breaking. Size 80/12 and 90/14 are your most frequently used needle sizes; stock up on them. Buy one package of 100/16 for heavier work and one package of 70/10 for finer work. The second number indicates the American numbering system and the first number the European system. Needles labeled H are all purpose for knits and woven fabrics. Ball-point needles are for knits. On Singer machines, try Singer Yellow brand and Red brand needles if you continue to have skipped-stitch problems. Test your stitch formation, stitch length, needle, and thread with every new project using a different fabric.

A *serger*, or overlock machine, is nice but not essential. Using three or four threads, it finishes edges and seams and knits woven fabrics. For a discussion on serging batting see the Note in Chapter 2 under Assembly of the Jacket.

Iron and ironing board. First on my Christmas list is an industrial-type iron and (better yet) a home press. They steam better than less-expensive irons.

Your ironing board needs to be well padded, and old wool blankets make good padding. Make your own cover from a heavy cotton, and use an old cover as a pattern.

Keep a spray bottle of water nearby if your iron doesn't steam well. Wrinkles in prewashed cottons need steam or water to disappear. Keep a spray bottle of vinegar and water handy as well. Vinegar helps remove hem lines and fold lines from fabrics.

Scissors. A minimum of three pairs of scissors are necessary: scissors for cutting paper; razor-sharp shears (7″ [17.5cm] or 8″ [20cm] with one handle larger than the other) for cutting fabric only; and small, sharp-pointed scissors for cutting threads and buttonholes.

Rotary cutter and mat board. Buy the largest healing mat board you can afford and your space allows. Some mat boards are marked with a grid and angle lines, which are helpful. Rotary cutters come in small and large sizes. Buy a large cutter and extra blades. Along with your sewing machine, the rotary cutter is a great labor saver. See Fig. 3-5 for setup.

Measuring equipment includes a wide Plexiglas ruler such as Omnigrid, 60″ (2.7m) fabric tape measure (with metal on both ends and numbers readable from both ends), a yardstick, and a 6″ (15cm) hem gauge with a slide for remembering your measurement. Measurements in this book are noted first in inches and then millimeters (mm), centimeters (cm), decimeters (dm), or meters (m).

A *seam ripper* will be helpful. The sewing machine companies make good, sharp rippers.

Pins. I use large glass-headed quilter's pins, which are easy to grip with my big hands. I find a pin inside the sandwiches of the clothing at times that I have to work out. Beware of the plastic-headed pins; I once ironed over one and could not remove the melted plastic from the garment. Use small pleating pins for silk and sheer fabric. Invest in a magnetic pin holder and a wrist pin cushion for fitting.

Hand sewing needles. Sharp size 7-through-10 needles are good choices for hand sewing. Size 10 is the smallest. Try a package of shorter quilter's needles called "betweens." Get an assortment until you find the smallest size you can thread easily.

Pattern weights are used to secure pattern pieces on fabric. They work much faster than pins. I used to laugh at a neighbor who used books to hold patterns in place.

Marking equipment includes a disappearing pen or blue wash-out pen, chalk, or a sliver of soap (depending on the color of the fabric). I wish the notion companies would invent marking equipment that we can be more confident using. The blue washable pens may leave color in the batting that will migrate to the surface years later. The disappearing pen's color returns when the fabric is pressed. Chemically, I'm not sure what either does to the fabric. After all of this, I use both types plus soap and the silver pens.

The brand-new Hera marker from Japan makes sharp lines on cotton and silk. It is a piece of plastic with a sharp edge that leaves a crease on the fabric and contains no chemicals. It is fine for simple designs (in Chapter 2) but not for more complicated designs. The mark is easier to see on solid colors than prints.

Seam sealant is a glue to keep stitches from pulling out in buttonholes and secure knots on the back of machine quilting. Fray Check is one brand.

Bias turners and makers. For turning bias cords one of the following is needed: Fasturn, bodkin, cord turner; or you can do it the hard way with a safety pin. For making folded bias use Fasturn or bias makers that come in various sizes. See Chapter 5 on the Koss appliqué method for details on using these products.

Design equipment (see Chapter 2's Design section).

Thread to match outer shell and lining. I prefer using Metrosene or Gutermann thread. These European threads are smooth and give less lint. Sometimes I use cheaper polyester-wrapped cotton thread and if the needle size is large enough, I have no trouble with fraying and breaking.

Fabrics.

1. For *outer shell fabrics,* 100-percent cotton is preferred, but I sometimes use blends. Ideally, you want a good-quality cotton of broadcloth weight. Poor-quality cotton has a loose weave (which can be detected by holding the fabric up to the light and looking for many air spaces and few threads) and excess sizing detected by rubbing the fabric together to see if powder comes out). Most cottons today are around 45″ (12.5m) wide and vary an inch or two depending on the width of the weaving machine. Buy some extra fabric or check widths at the store. A friend of mine who is new to quilting was annoyed to have to purchase more of one fabric for a quilt she was making because the fabric widths listed in her instructions and what was available in the store were different.

Consider looking at flea markets and yard sales for interesting fabrics.

Stop at the washing machine when you come in the door with any fabric purchase, zipper, tapes and some of the interfacings (not fusible!) you buy. I wash light colors with a light load of regular wash and darks with a dark load. I often will test the dark fabrics again in hot water, as there tend to be excessive dyes in the dark colors. Some quilters add vinegar to set the dye. Hand-wash colored silks separately. Dark-colored silks bleed dye each time they are washed.

2. *Lining fabrics.* I again recommend cottons (to keep the garment all natural), but sometimes I use a polyester lining. Stay away from acetate linings that wear quickly.

3. *Backing fabric.* Use 6 yds. (5.4m) (3 yds. [2.7m] for jacket) of an old, prewashed material as a backing fabric. Old sheets, cheap fabric from an outlet, or a fabric you'll never use elsewhere are all handy. (Start a pile of such fabrics.) In this coat the color of the backing does not have to be white, as it will later when you must work with white or off-white. This is a good place to use that print you don't know why you bought.

Batting. Use 2-½ yds. (2.2m) of batting for a jacket. Your choices follow, and include resources listed in the Bibliography and under Sources of Fabrics.

1. Prewashed cotton flannel provides a cooler jacket for summer and not much quilting definition.

2. Cotton batting needs to be quilted with stitches 2″ (5cm) apart to prevent shifting. It is not suitable for machine quilting unless you will be doing *a lot* of quilting. There is not enough loft for dense quilting.

3. Light quilting batting, sometimes called "low loft," is 100-percent polyester-bonded (a glazene finish), which prevents fibers from migrating through your fabric. This weight is available in many bed sizes and is a good choice for the projects in this book. A crib size is enough for one jacket. Sometimes it is found by the yard, which is an economical buy.

4. Traditional polyester bonded batting has all the characteristics of light quilting batting but is slightly heavier. This is my usual choice.

5. Fat batt or extra-loft batting has the same characteristics as light quilting batting but is heavier. Quilters use this batt for tying quilts. It works well with our projects if you use a simple quilt pattern and want a warmer garment.

6. Cotton classic (cotton and polyester) should be preshrunk (a step I'm not willing to do).

7. Thermore and needle punch battings are 100-percent polyester battings, but thinner and stiffer. I find them too stiff and ungiving.

■ Necessary Sewing Skills

Fitting and Making a Muslin

If you plan to sew many clothes for yourself and a regular pattern does not fit or you aren't sure what size to buy, *don't skip this step.* Go to your home-extension sewing specialist, a fabric store, or an experienced seamstress in your area to help you take your measurements and decide the correct pattern size with which to start. Buy a basic pattern such as McCall's 2718 produced in cooperation with Palmer/Pletsch. (Order it through the store where you purchase patterns.) Go home and cut it out of muslin or gingham check. The check helps align the straights of grain correctly. If the checks are crooked on your body, you know you need to adjust in that area. Go back to your helper and have her fit the muslin. This is a step in sewing we often neglect, but it makes the difference between a garment looking amateurish or professionally made. From now on, at least until your weight changes, you can purchase the correct pattern size and use your muslin to make adjustments.

Pattern, Layout, and Cutting

Work on the dining room table, a large work table, or the floor for laying out and cutting your pattern. Dining table protectors placed upside down will keep the fabric from slipping. A cardboard cutting board is helpful but not essential; a bed is not firm enough and is hard on your back. Press pattern pieces with a warm iron if they are wrinkled. Fabric should be pressed and folded lengthwise with the selvages together. Right sides of the fabric are usually folded to the inside.

Have pattern weights, scissors, and a yardstick or tape measure handy. The yardstick is used to check the grain of the fabric by measuring in two places from the pattern grainline arrow to the selvage edge of the fabric. If the measurements are the same, your pattern is positioned correctly. I usually put two pins at the ends of the arrows to hold the pattern on the fabric on grain.

The pattern instruction sheet will assist you in arranging the pattern pieces on the fabric. Arrange your pattern pieces and put weights at the corners. Cut with your right hand while holding the pattern and fabric flat with your left hand. Do the reverse if you are left-handed. Mark notches by snipping straight into the area $\frac{1}{8}''$ (3mm) once for a single notch and twice for a double notch. If you need all of the seam allowance for fitting, or if you are making French seams, cut outward around the notches. Be sure to mark center sleeves and center fronts with snips. You also could use your rotary cutter and mat.

Hint: To consolidate cutting, cut several garments at one time. As long as you are making a mess, make a good one. A friend on the other side of the table with shears in hand is a big help. Pile all cut pattern pieces and notions for one project in a separate box or basket. Next, go through the pieces you have just cut and mark each one if you didn't do so as you cut them.

Continuous Sewing

Continuous sewing saves you time and frustration. See Fig. 1-1. Count how many stops and starts it takes to remove fabric from the machine, cut the thread, and start again, and think of the mishaps that can happen along the way. Instead, sew continuously using the following directions. When sewing similar pieces together, sew one

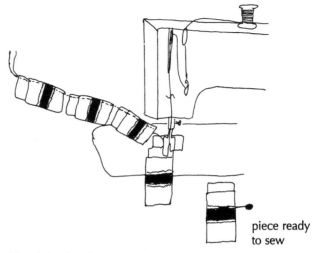

piece ready to sew

Fig. 1-1. *Continuous sewing.*

unit, but do not cut the thread or lift the presser foot. Sew on air for a stitch or two, then insert the next unit and continue to sew. Continue in this manner until all units are sewn, then cut the units apart. Quilter Georgia Bonesteel calls this setting up a "mini factory." We use it in sewing Seminole segments together, but there are other places you can sew this way as well. For example, sew one shoulder seam, pull the second shoulder seam over, and sew without cutting the thread.

Consolidated Sewing

This is a second time-saver. Consolidated sewing refers to grouping all of the sewing you can sew at one time on a garment while at the machine, and then getting up, pressing, pinning, and grouping the next units to be sewn before sitting at the machine again. Here's how to group the sewing on the dense machine-quilted jacket you'll sew in Chapter 6. Beside your machine, stack the two outer sleeves, two lining sleeves, lining fronts pinned to the lining back, and outer-shell fronts pinned to outer-shell back. Sew separate shoulder seams on the lining and outer shell, set the machine for gathering, and sew gathering rows in all four sleeves. Get up, press shoulder seams, and pin sleeves into the back/front units. Sit at the machine again and sew the final two rows for each sleeve and long under arm/side

BASIC SEWING TECHNIQUES FOR MACHINE QUILTING

seam of the outer shell and lining before getting up again. A little thought and organization gets the job done. Turn the telephone off to prevent disturbances. Some sewers lower their ironing board and place it near the sewing machine so they do not have to get up. I get restless after sitting for too long.

Staystitching

Staystitching is a row of stitching $\frac{1}{2}''$ (1.3cm) from the edge of curved sections of the garment that is sewn before construction begins. See Fig. 1-2. The purpose of staystitching is to hold the curved (bias) areas firmly during construction. You sew *with* the grain. Sewing *against* the grain raises and loosens threads. On a neckline, for example, sew from one shoulder to the middle of the piece, then start at the other shoulder and sew to the middle. Pattern direction sheets pro-

Fig. 1-2. *Staystitching. Stitch in the direction of the arrows.*

vide illustrations for the direction to sew and list the garment pieces in the pattern that need to be staystitched.

French Seams

French seams are a method of finishing seams on lighter weight fabrics such as broadcloth (which is the weight I use in the skirts in the final chapter). See Fig. 1-3. The raw edges of the seam are enclosed completely so no fraying occurs when the skirt is washed, and the inside of the skirt looks neat (which is important when sewing for other people). French seams require sewing the seam twice. First, stitch a $\frac{1}{2}''$ (1.3cm) seam with the *wrong* sides together. Stitch from the bottom of the skirt to the top (with the grain again). Press the seam flat to set the stitches. Trim the seam to $\frac{1}{4}''$ (6mm). Fold on the exact seam line with the *correct* sides together. Stitch a second time just a fraction past your first row of stitching. On sheer fabrics you can make the seam narrower. No ravels should show from the front of the seam.

Darts

See the section entitled Quilted Jackets for the Larger Figure in Chapter 7 for information on

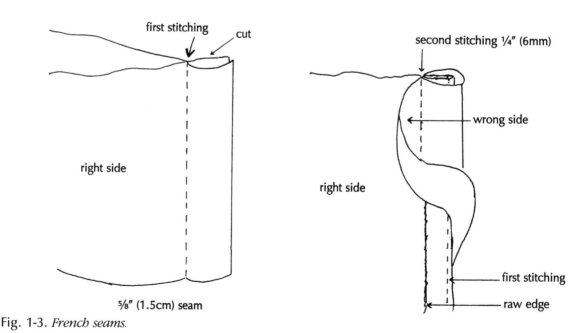

Fig. 1-3. *French seams.*

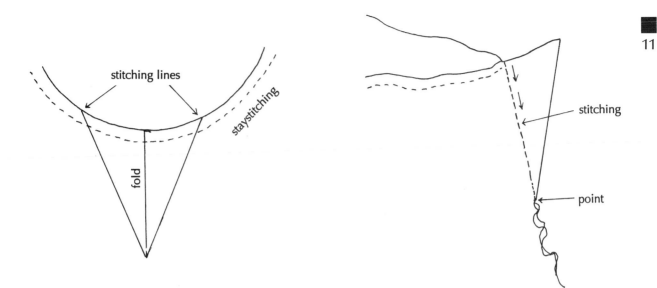

Fig. 1-4. *Creating a dart.*

changing the pattern dart. See Fig. 1-4 for information on making a dart.

A dart gives shape to a garment so that it fits the contours of the body. Darts are usually a wide fold at the edge of the garment that narrow to nothing in the body of the garment. Pin and mark the stitching line by stretching transparent tape against, not on, the stitching line. Stitch from the wide part of the dart to the narrow part. As you approach the narrow end, shorten the machine stitch length and stitch the last few stitches parallel to the fold one thread away from the fold. Do not backstitch. Instead, either tie the threads or sew on air with the machine and dab seam sealant on the thread ends beside the point of the dart.

Gathering

Gathering is another way to give ease to a garment to fit the contours of the body. See Fig. 1-5. Darts in skirts and at shoulders can be transformed to gathering for a softer look. We use

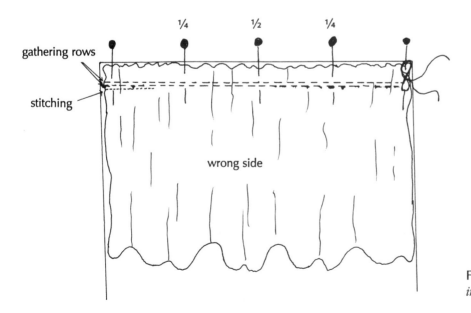

Fig. 1-5. *Gathering pinned in place.*

gathering to make two of the skirts described in the final chapter.

Two rows of the largest stitch your machine makes (not the basting stitch on computer sewing machines) are sewn within the seam allowance in the area to be gathered. The usual distances are $\frac{1}{2}''$ (1.3cm) and $\frac{5}{8}''$ (2cm) from the edge. Pin the right side of the gathered piece to the right side of the waistband and pin at all marks. If the skirt is not marked, divide each piece in half and fourths and pin. Pull up the gathers to match the waistband and pin the divisions. It is easier to pull the bobbin thread. Secure thread ends by wrapping them around a pin and distribute the gathers evenly. Shorten the stitch length and final-stitch from the gathering side one thread beyond the deepest gathering row. Hold the gathers straight out to the left side as you stitch so you won't catch tucks in the seamline. Grade the seam and cut the gathering side narrower. Press upward.

Blind Machine Hemming

The blind-hemfoot is a very useful, time-saving attachment for hemming a straight skirt. See Fig. 1-6. Use the smallest machine needle and finest thread compatible with your fabric to make a stitch that just catches the hem. Mark your hem, press, and finish the edge with the serger or a zigzag stitch on your regular machine. Pin the hem. Baste through all layers with the sewing machine (optional). Fold the hem so the right side of the hem is on the right side of the skirt. Leave the hem edge exposed $\frac{1}{4}''$ (6mm). Place the blind-hem attachment on the machine and set the machine for blind hemming. Practice on a scrap of the same fabric as your garment. The guide follows along on the edge of the fold. Stitch slowly and evenly, just catching a thread or two of the hem. It may be necessary to move the stitch width and length. If the stitch seems tight when you open up the hem, loosen the top tension. When you are pleased, sew the skirt. Remove the basting and press the bottom of the hem.

Top Stitching

Top stitching helps hold seams in place and is decorative. Top stitching shows and should be sewn carefully. Use a matching thread, a heavier thread, or even two threads through the same needle. You may need a heavier needle than your 100/16 needle, and there are special top-stitching needles on the market that have longer shanks. Either mark the line to be sewn with transparent tape or chalk, use the quilting guide or the side of the presser foot as a guide. I often use my blind-hem foot and move the needle to the left when top-stitching the vests. The machine is set for straight stitching. Be sure your bobbin and upper threads are full so you won't have to stop and start in the middle of a row. On garments with

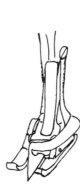

blind hemmer foot

Fig. 1-6. *Blind hemming.*

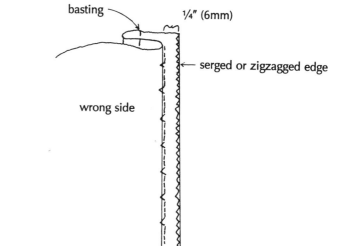

basting

¼″ (6mm)

← serged or zigzagged edge

wrong side

nap or loose grain, it's a good idea to stitch in the same direction. Hence, if you stitch one front from the bottom to the top, stitch the other front from the same direction. Stitch slowly and evenly. As with any procedure, test before you begin.

Clipping and Grading

Clipping is cutting into a seam allowance $\frac{1}{2}''$ (1.3cm) at a right angle to the seam stitching. See Fig. 1-7. The purpose of clipping is to open a curved area so the area can be reversed smoothly or clipped to allow another piece to be added as a straight seam. An example of the latter is when clipping the neck edge to add a collar. Staystitching prevents the seam from pulling and fraying. An inward curve is clipped as described; an outward curve is clipped to remove v-shaped pieces.

Grading is cutting a seam parallel to the seam stitching in order to reduce seam bulk. The seam allowance that will lie next to the outside garment piece is kept longer, and the seam allowance that will be inside is cut shorter. This grading makes the seam flat and less noticeable from the top side when the garment is pressed.

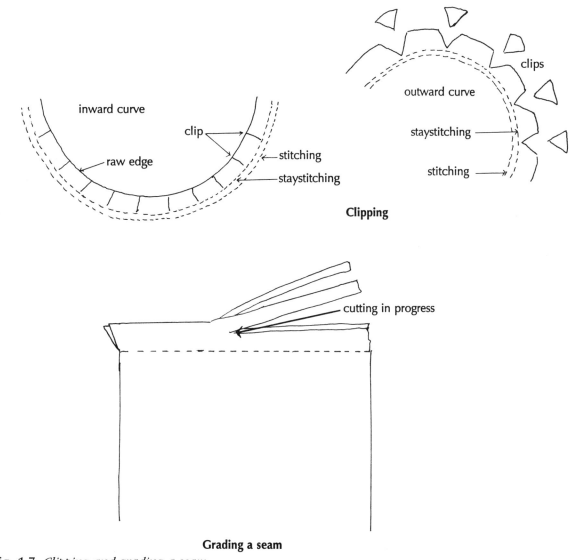

Clipping

Grading a seam

Fig. 1-7. *Clipping and grading a seam.*

Setting in Sleeves

Setting in a sleeve in the method described under Assembly of the Jacket in Chapter 2 is the easiest way to sew the sleeve. The method can be adapted to other garments. The reason for ease in the sleeve is to give the arm and shoulder room to move while keeping the fabric on the fronts and back near the body. Practice this method and sleeves will become easy for you to do.

Zippers

I prefer inserting zippers for skirts in the back seam. See Fig. 1-8. Purchase your zipper 2″ (5cm) longer than the zipper opening. Machine-baste the zipper opening closed. Press the seam open. From the underside, position the zipper face-down in the center of the back-basted seam. Tape the zipper in position with transparent tape. The excess zipper will be above the seam, and the zipper slide is at the top of the zipper. Having a longer zipper prevents a bump when you sew around the slide. You may want to mark your stitching line with transparent tape on the front. Attach your machine zipper foot and stitch from the front side. Remove tape and basting stitches and push the zipper slide toward the bottom of the zipper. You can cut the tops of the zipper, but save a small amount to finish in the waistband seam. Beware: If you try on the skirt before you've put on the waistband and after you've trimmed the zipper top, the slider will come off. You can fix it by prying off the stop at the bottom and sliding it on again.

Waistbands

Measure your waistline. See Fig. 1-9. Add 3″ (7.5cm) for lapped-end and seam allowances to that measurement. The usual width is 3-¾″ (9.5cm), while results in a waistband width of 1-¼″ (3cm). You can adjust the width measurement to your liking.

Cut the waistband with one long edge on the selvage for the inside of the band. The selvage will finish the inside seam and replace bulk that results from turning under the inside seam.

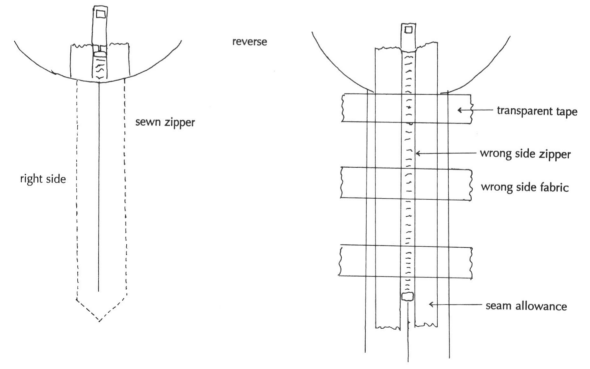

Fig. 1-8. *Setup for stitching a zipper.*

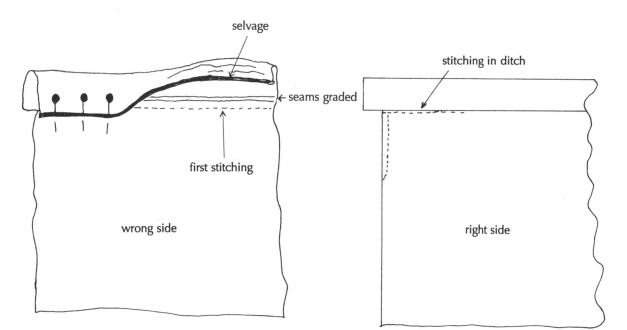

Fig. 1-9. *Stitching a waistband.*

Lay the waistband wrong side up on the ironing board and bond it with a waist shaper. The waist shaper is cut to the exact waist measurement. Pin the ends of the waistband right sides together and stitch across the ends. Grade the seam and clip the upper corner. Reverse and press. Pin to the waist, right sides together; match center front and side seams; and leave 2″ (5cm) over the edge on one end and nothing overlapped at the other end. The overlap forms a placket to which you will later sew an eye fastener. Stitch. Grade the seam. Press toward the waistband. Pin the back of the waistband. From the front stitch in the ditch, close to the fold of the band, but stitch on the skirt side. Smaller stitches will make the stitches less visible. You are catching the underlap of the band. This is a very good place to use the even-feed foot to keep the layers together evenly. Top-stitch the waistband if desired.

Buttonholes

For making machine-made buttonholes, use the finest needle and thread compatible with your fabric. Cotton thread makes good buttonholes and fills in better than cotton-wrapped polyester. Buttonholes, like satin stitches and densely formed program stitches, need stabilizing to form well. Use tear-away, fusible interfacing or scraps of the same fabric. When we make quilted jackets, the batting provides enough stabilization. Mark your buttonhole with a disappearing pencil, transparent tape, soap, or hand baste.

Horizontal buttonholes start $\frac{1}{2}$″ (1.3cm) from the edge or $\frac{1}{8}$″ (3mm) out toward the front edge from the center front. Measure your button by folding a piece of tape around its widest part and use one half of that measurement. On thicker fabrics such as our quilted garments, you may want to increase the measurement a bit. Practice on scrap fabric (similar to your jacket) first. Stitch buttonholes. Place a small amount of seam sealant on the back of the buttonhole. Let the sealant dry and then cut your buttonhole. If using the semi-automatic buttonhole maker, you can restitch the buttonholes to cover better. Review the use of the buttonhole maker that comes with your machine in your instruction book.

Cutting Bias

Bias is a 45-degree line on a piece of fabric. See Fig. 2-16. The advantages of using bias is its greater stretch and lesser likelihood of raveling.

We want the bias to be smooth around curved edges. In a woven fabric the true bias is formed when the cross grain (from selvage to selvage) is folded exactly parallel to the lengthwise grain (along the selvage). One half of a yard of 45" (12.5m) fabric is a good amount with which to work. Save the leftover fabric for use as bias in another project or as scraps in piecing. I have a box of bias pieces that comes in handy when I need to finish a pot holder or bib.

Once you get your bias fold, press carefully to avoid stretching. Slit the pressed line with your scissors or open up the fold and cut with scissors. Align the two bias edges together again and fold the tails in to make six layers of bias fabric with one even edge. Press the folds so no bows result when cutting. Use your rotary cutter and healing mat to cut. Place the fabric on the cutting mat, align it with your Plexiglas ruler, and cut the desired width. Piece and then press the open-pieced seams. Your bias is ready to use.

In Chapter 5 sections on the Koss Method of Appliqué and piping and cording, I will show you more uses for bias.

■ Resources

Books by Bishop, Brown, Ladbury, Palmer, Saunders, Shaeffer, Singer, Vogue, and Zieman will help you with basic sewing skills. See complete listings in the Bibliography.

Other sources of help are magazines published by pattern and sewing machine dealers, and magazines such as *Threads* and *Sew News.* An increasing number of videos are available for rent or purchase. Classes taken at sewing machine dealers, technical schools, home extension programs, fabric companies, and adult home economics programs are further possibilities for help. Get together with friends and share knowledge. A group of young mothers in my community meets once a month to learn from one another. They recently took a trip to Washington, D.C., to G Street Fabrics to learn and increase their fabric stashes.

CHAPTER 2

Easy Quilted Jacket Made from One Fabric

First, we shall make an easy jacket using one fabric for the outer shell. Then we'll quilt it with the machine, either with the feed dogs up or free motion. This is the easiest jacket to make and a good place to start if you have not machine-quilted garments previously. Your jacket will be very useful to wear in spring or fall as an outer jacket and, depending on the fabric, either can be dressy or worn with jeans. Construction of this jacket does not require knowledge of tailoring. I have only tailored one jacket in my life, but I've made hundreds of quilted jackets. See the lavender jacket in the color section and Fig. 2-1.

Some of my students like to plunge right into a jacket and some prefer to make a practice piece first. A 16″ (40cm) square of cotton is a good size for practice. Follow the directions for making a sandwich, designing, marking, and machine-quilting your piece. If your square pleases you, it can be sewn into a pillow or large tote.

Shopping List

Let's review the list of materials from Chapter 1 and make some additions and changes for the easy quilted jacket.

☐ A commercial pattern with few seams, no darts, and set-in sleeves. Buy a size ample enough for you. (See special section in Chapter 7 for larger sizes.) The size needs to be ample not only to allow for quilting shrinkage but also to allow the jacket to be worn over a sweater.

☐ Use 2-½ yds. (2.2m) of 45″ (1.2m) wide fabric. Your choices are many—100-percent cotton, a blend of polyester and cotton (no more than 40-percent polyester), hand-dyed fabric, drapery fabric, velveteen, corduroy, lightweight wool, or wool blend. You want the fabric soft

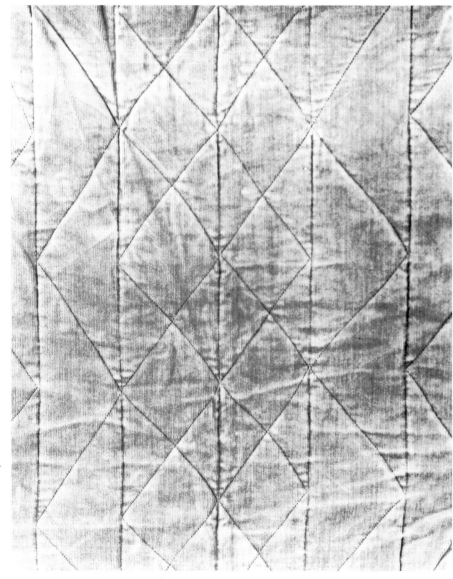

Fig. 2-1. *Close-up of brown cut corduroy jacket, one of my first jackets. This was made of one fabric, using cardboard templates in geometric shapes to draw the quilting design. 1982. Owner: Dot Michaels.*

enough to puff with the quilting. Fabric such as denim is too stiff. Stay away from silks and slick fabrics until you have experience quilting on the machine.

Hint: Lately I've been using more drapery fabrics, which are easy to find in my area in interesting larger-scale prints. I order cottons and other fabrics from companies listed in the Bibliography. I have found prices reasonable, quality high, and delivery prompt.

☐ Use 2-½ yds. (2.2m) of matching or correlating fabric for the lining. Cotton is best here. A small print is good for a beginner since stitches will be somewhat hidden in the print.

☐ Use 2-½ yds. (2.2m) of batting. Your choices follow, and include resources listed in the Bibliography and under Sources of Fabrics.

1. Prewashed cotton flannel provides a cooler jacket for summer and not much quilting definition.

2. Cotton batting needs to be quilted with stitches 2″ (5cm) apart to prevent shifting. It is not suitable for machine quilting unless you will be doing *a lot* of quilting. There is not enough loft for dense quilting.

3. Light quilting batting, sometimes called "low loft," is 100-percent polyester-bonded (a glazene finish), which prevents fibers from migrating through your fabric. This weight is available in many bed sizes and is a good choice for the projects in this book. A crib size is enough for one jacket. Sometimes it is found by the yard, which is an economical buy.

4. Traditional batting has all the characteristics of light quilting batting but is slightly heavier. This is my usual choice.

5. Fat batt or extra-loft batting has the same characteristics as light quilting batting but is heavier. Quilters use this batt for tying quilts. It works well with our projects if you use a simple quilt pattern and want a warmer garment.

6. Cotton classic (cotton and polyester) should be preshrunk (a step I'm not willing to do).

7. Thermore and needle pounch battings are 100-percent polyester battings, but thinner and stiffer. I find them too stiff and ungiving.

See Figs. 2-2 and 2-3. The summer jacket in Fig. 2-2 has cotton flannel for batting, and lighter batting is in Fig. 2-3. I don't enjoy using either.

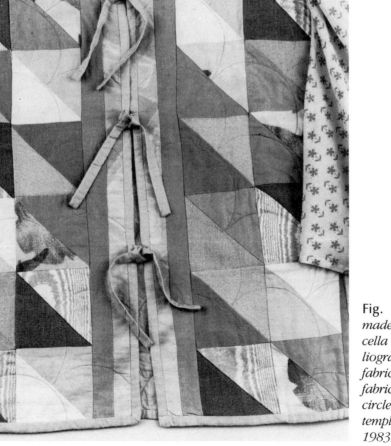

Fig. 2-2. *Summer jacket made with an Yvonne Porcella pattern (see the Bibliography), Procion-dyed fabric, linens and decorator fabrics, flannel batting, half-circle quilting drawn with a template, and feed dogs up. 1983.*

EASY QUILTED JACKET MADE FROM ONE FABRIC

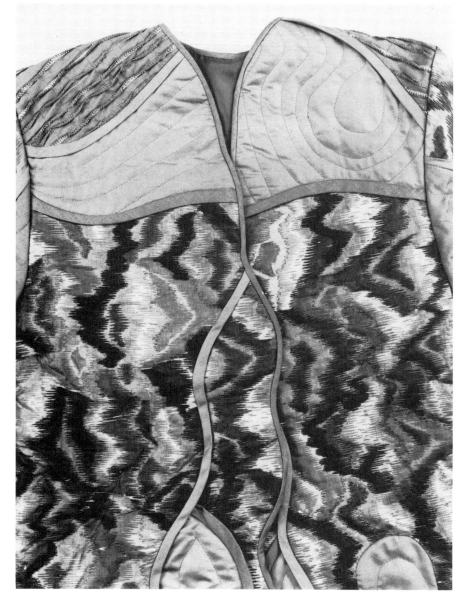

Fig. 2-3. *Curved pieced jacket in Lois Ericson style (see the Bibliography) with tucks stitched with fancy threads done on a serger, folded bias in seams, polyester lining, and curved front edges. Quilted to batting with invisible thread. Design follows the pattern of the print; feed dogs down. 1983.*

☐ Use ½ yd. (.5m) outside or lining fabric for bias trim.

☐ Thread to match outer shell and lining. I prefer using Metrosene or Gutermann thread. These European threads are smooth and give less lint. Sometimes I use cheaper polyester-wrapped cotton thread and if the needle size is large enough, I have no trouble with fraying and breaking.

☐ Marking equipment includes a disappearing pen or blue wash-out pen, chalk, or a sliver of soap (depending on the color of the fabric). I wish the notion companies would invent marking equipment that we can be more confident using. The blue washable pens may leave color in the batting that will migrate to the surface years later. The disappearing pen's color returns when the fabric is pressed. Chemically, I'm not sure what either does to the fabric. After all of this, I use both types plus soap and the silver pens.

The brand-new Hera marker from Japan makes sharp lines on cotton and silk. It is a piece of plastic with a sharp edge that leaves a crease on the fabric and contains no chemicals. It is fine for simple designs (in Chapter 2) but not for more complicated designs. The mark is easier to see on solid colors than prints.

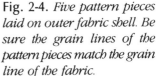☐ A sewing machine well-oiled and free of lint. A serger symbol will be used in the margin of the text when you can use a four-thread serger. The serger saves time and neatens seams at the same time. I'm marking seams to serge to remind myself as well as you. After years of sewing on a regular machine, I can easily forget to serge. Thread your serger with compatible thread when you start a new project so you'll be ready to switch to serging when appropriate. I like to use woolly nylon in the loopers for a softer seam coverage.

☐ An even-feed or walking foot for your machine

is very helpful. Consider investing if you plan much machine quilting.

☐ Machine needle the proper size for the weight of fabric and the thread thickness. I use an 80/12 size needle with cottons with and without batting. With corduroy use a jeans needle or size 100/16.

■ Setting Up for the Design

Preshrink all fabrics. Press.

Using only five pattern pieces—two sleeves, back, and two fronts—cut your outer fabric shell. See Fig. 2-4. Cut ½″ (1.3cm) larger around all pattern pieces to allow for quilting shrinkage. Be sure nap fabrics are going one way. Cut lining 2″

Outer Fabric Shell

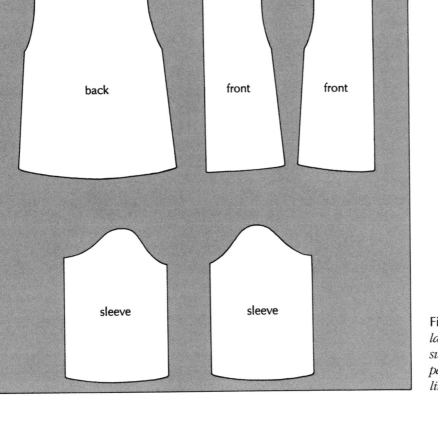

Fig. 2-4. *Five pattern pieces laid on outer fabric shell. Be sure the grain lines of the pattern pieces match the grain line of the fabric.*

(5cm) longer than the shell. Cut batting from lining pieces. Mark sleeve center and notches. Collar, pocket, and bias will be cut later.

Press outer shell and lining fabrics. This is your last chance to press because pressing fabric with batting inside will bond the batting to your fabrics.

Hint: Keep a spray bottle of water by your iron to spray cottons and other wrinkly fabrics. I still sprinkle some linens and cottons and wrap them in a towel as my mother did. Ironing is not that awful. Jan Saunders' book *Sew, Serge, Press: Speed Tailoring in the Ultimate Sewing Center* (listed in the Bibliography) is a wonderful resource on pressing and ironing. The book reminds me of what my mother always told me about the importance of pressing while sewing. She learned by the Bishop sewing method (noted in the Bibliography), which emphasizes pressing with the correct equipment.

■ Design

The following equipment (shown in Fig. 2-5) is helpful in designing: yardstick, flexible curve, Plexiglas quilter's templates, right angle, dressmaker's curve, compass, large sheets of light-colored paper, lightweight cardboard (cereal box weight), pencils, and permanent markers.

Hint: Keep your drawing equipment with your sewing supplies, ready to use. Save designs you make for use at another time. I go back today and find work I did years ago very helpful. My designs are stored in files marked Flowers, Birds, etc.

The rules for the design you will draw are: 1) lines start at top and go to the bottom of jacket; 2) lines do not cross one another more than once; 3) lines are no more than 3" (7.5cm) apart and no less than 1" (2.5cm) apart; 4) no stopping and starting in the middle.

These rules are for beginners. Later you will learn how to break some of them. You can plan to use your machine either under control (feed

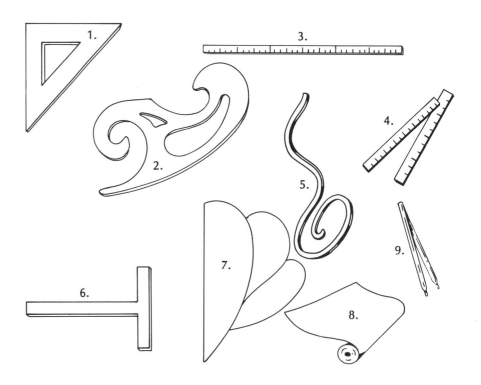

Fig. 2-5. *Tools used for designing: 1) triangle, 2) French curve, 3) yardstick, 4) ruler, 5) flexible curve, 6) T-square, 7) dressmaker's curve, 8) paper, 9) pencils and pens. Collect and keep these tools in your sewing area.*

dogs up) or free motion (see Chapter 6 on dense stitching for free-motion setup).

See examples of designs in Fig. 2-6 and in the photographs of jackets at the beginning of the chapter. Plan your design on sheets of paper (to match your jacket parts) or directly on the fabric pieces. Make templates from lightweight cardboard, being sure to cut just one side of the design. See Fig. 2-7 for examples of templates. Your fabric may have a print that you can follow and quilt around (see Fig. 2-8). In such a case you may choose to use invisible thread, which comes in clear for light fabrics and smoke for dark fabrics. The new invisible threads (.004mm fine [See Clotilde's in the Supply List. YLI makes #80 and #60, with #60 the finer.]) are soft and work well in the sewing machine. Be careful with the size of invisible thread you purchase, because some of the old, heavier threads still are in the stores.

Mark your design on the jacket parts with the appropriate marking pencil.

■ Fabric Sandwiches

Make five fabric sandwiches of the pattern pieces you have cut out. Place the lining on your work area right-side-down. Lay the batting on top, then place the marked outer shell piece right-side-up. Be sure to reverse one sleeve and one front piece.

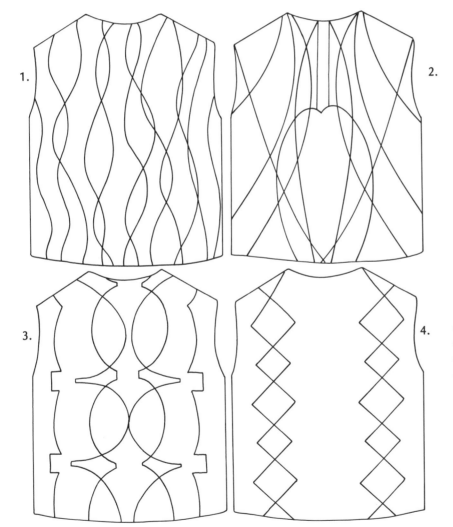

Fig. 2-6. Designs for quilting a one-fabric jacket. Shown are the backs of jackets: 1) drawn with a flexible curve, 2) drawn with a dressmaker's curve, 3) and 4) drawn with a template. Use the same design for the front and elements of the design for the sleeves. It is not necessary to draw and keep all five pieces. Make up designs for yourself and follow the rules in the text.

EASY QUILTED JACKET MADE FROM ONE FABRIC

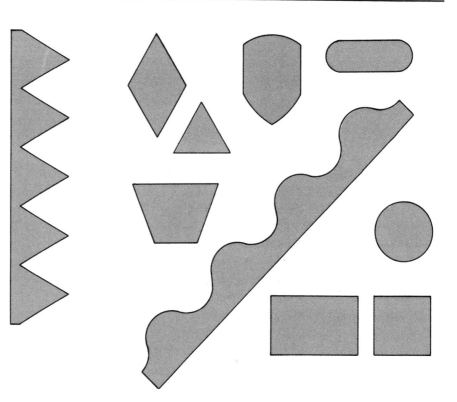

Fig. 2-7. *Assorted templates made of lightweight cardboard. Notice that some are drawn on only one side of the template material so they do not fall apart. Collect and save these.*

Start

Fig. 2-8. *Quilting around a print. A printed fabric gives you a design to follow. Just find a path through the print from top to bottom and stitch.*

Pin all around the edges, about 4″ (10cm) apart. No basting is necessary. See Fig. 2-9.

■ Quilting

Thread your machine with the appropriate color of thread. Attach the even-feed foot, if using one, or darning foot if you are free-motion quilting. Using 10 to 14 (2mm) stitches per inch is fine. Use needle-down position if your machine has it. Start sewing at top center of one jacket piece. Let your hands pull very gently on each side of the needle with the fabric grain as the fabric goes through the machine. Your hands are flat and comfortably relaxed on the bed of the machine.

Start the second row from the top again, next to the center row. Continue working out from the center on each side. Check the back of the sandwich to see if there are puckers on the lining. If you find puckers, rip them out, smooth the fabric, repin, and try again. Pins will have to be repositioned part-way through sewing a section of jacket. Check and reposition if necessary. You can see the sides are beginning to bow where the pins

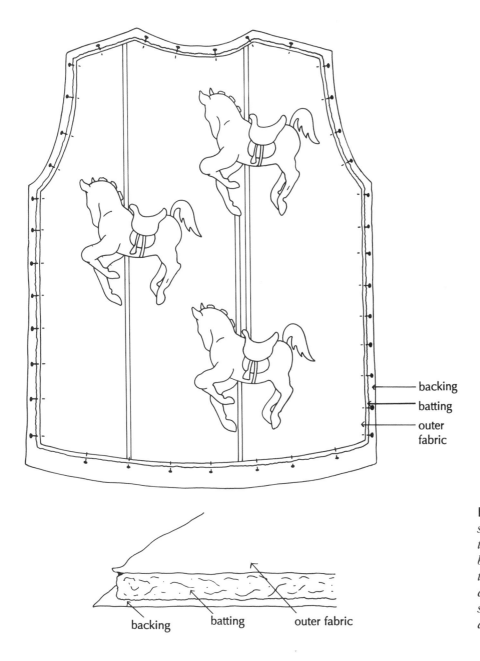

backing
batting
outer fabric

Fig. 2-9. *Making your fabric sandwich. The lining is on the bottom right-side-down, batting and outer fabric on the top right-side-up, and the design drawn on the top right side. The sandwich is pinned and ready to quilt.*

backing   batting   outer fabric

are placed. Without an even-feed foot, the lining will draw up some—and that is the reason for the extra lining at the bottom. Before I knew this, the first jacket I machine quilted ended with the lining 2″ (5cm) up the back, which I compensated for with an extra wide bias trim—not too swift. When finished quilting the five pieces, trim the batting and lining to match the outer shell. The batting will have pushed out from the sandwich.

■ Fitting

Now is a good time to have a friend help you fit your jacket. Pin the shoulder and side seams. Check the shoulder seam: Pin in spare shoulder pads if you use them. Check the length; adjust. Check the back for bulging at the bottom: This can be adjusted by taking in the back at the sides. Pin in the sleeve and determine length and fit of the armhole. Remember, unlike a suit jacket, a quilted jacket is not a tightly fitted garment. You will want enough room to wear a sweater under the jacket. Make sure the side seams of the back are equal to the side seams of the front. Round the front bottom edges for a softer look.

■ Assembly of the Jacket

Your quilting is finished, fitting is checked, and now you are ready to put your jacket together.

Seam Finishing Strips

Cut 1-½″ (3.8cm) strips on the straight grain of the lining fabric, cutting enough length for the side, sleeve, shoulder, and armhole seams. Lay these strips aside ready to sew in when seams are sewn.

Note: An alternative is to use finishing strips on the outside of the jacket with a contrasting fabric (sew seams with wrong sides together) or use a contrasting fabric on the inside. When you see a contrasting fabric finishing my seams, you know I was short on lining fabric. Any way you choose to do it, your jacket will be completely reversible.

Shoulder Seam

Change to a heavier needle (100/16) to sew through the multiple layers. Use a ⅝″ (1.5cm) seam allowance. Pin the right sides of the shoulder seams together. Pin finishing strip in place right-side-down on top of the wrong side of the front jacket shoulder seam. Stitch with a ⅝″ (1.5cm) seam. The needle-down position helps keep this seam from wavering as you sew. See Fig. 2-10 for the setup. Trim the seam with the jacket back seam allowance narrower than the front jacket seam allowance. Finger-press and pin the finishing strip toward the jacket back and turn under ½″ (1.3cm) of the strip to make a neat finish. You will hand-sew the strip later, but you need them in position

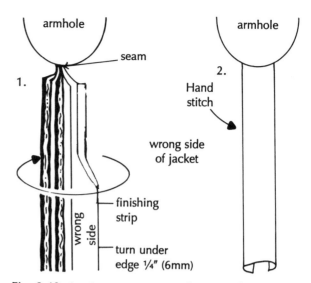

Fig. 2-10. *Sewing an extra strip for seam finish. 1. Sew a seam of the jacket together with a finishing strip in place. 2. Hand-stitch the second side of the finishing strip in place and fold under the seam allowance.*

and pinned now in order to complete the remainder of the jacket.

Note: I have changed my mind about using the serger when batting is in the seam. Do not serge. The serger knife may not cut the sandwich well or the batting in the sandwich may catch the serger finger, easily breaking it. If batting is absent in the seam or the batting is stitched down, the serger can handle the seam. On smaller items, Press-On Fleece can be used and works with the serger. I have just found another idea for dealing with a thick seam in the serger. *Know Your Serger*, a booklet from *Update Newsletters* (listed in the Bibliography), recommends zigzagging a heavy seam before serging.

I have used the lapped quilting method for finishing seams (see *Lap Quilting with Georgia Bonesteel* in the Bibliography), but I don't recommend the method for clothing because it is difficult to plan designs that are not quilted into the seam allowances. In lap quilting the finished seam allowance is left open. The outer shell seam allowances are sewn right sides together on the sewing machine. The piece is turned to the back and excess batting is trimmed so the batting butts together in the seam allowance. One lining seam allowance is smoothed over the other and turned under to form a narrow seam, then hand-stitched in place. This method produces a flatter, less bulky seam.

Sleeves

Sew two rows of gathering stitches between the notches over the cap on both sleeves, starting the first row $\frac{1}{2}''$ (1.3cm) from the edge and the second row $\frac{1}{8}''$ (3mm) from the first row of stitching.

Pin the sleeve to the jacket, right sides together, matching center notch and side notches of the sleeve to the jacket body. Place pins on the sleeve side of the seam where you will sew. Placing pins on the sewing side makes it easier to see pins and remove them as you sew.

Ease in fullness. Wrap your gathering threads around a pin in a figure-eight configuration at the

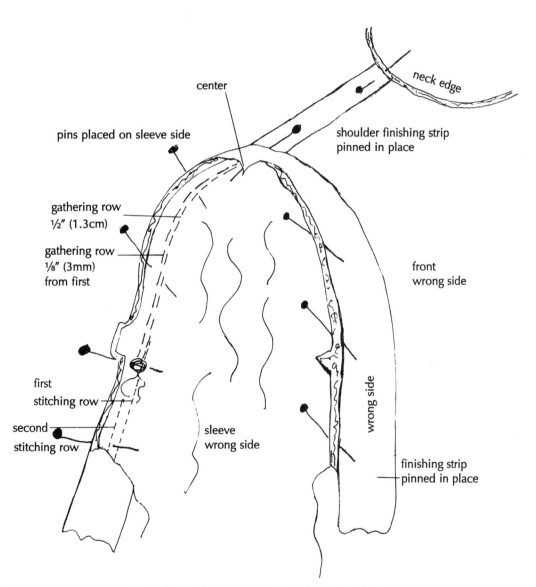

Fig. 2-11. *Sewing a sleeve together. The finishing strip can be added with the first sewing or an additional sewing. Sew from the sleeve side. Notice the position of the pins, the two gathering rows, and the two rows of stitching. After the final stitching, trim and push the seam toward the sleeve.*

EASY QUILTED JACKET MADE FROM ONE FABRIC

notches. This holds the ease in place until it is stitched.

Stitch with the sleeve side up one thread away from $\frac{1}{2}''$ gathering row. You can sew a finishing strip in on the bottom of that seam the first time around, or if you feel more sure, sew the seam a second time with the right side of the strip to the wrong side of jacket body (*not* on the sleeve side). Lift the work, peek, and reposition the strip as you sew. See Fig. 2-11.

Check the stitching from the front. If all is smooth with no unwanted puckers, sew again $\frac{1}{4}''$ (6mm) in from the previous stitching. Trim the seam. Push the seam toward the sleeve, fold finishing strip over the seam, turn under $\frac{1}{2}''$ (1.3cm) of strip, and pin in place at end of the seams.

Underarm and Side Seams

Sew the long seam of the sleeve and the jacket side with a finishing strip in place, matching the underarm carefully. Stitch slowly over the underarm seam. You may want to reinforce the underarm area with a second row of stitching. Pin finishing strips in place at the sleeve hem and the bottom of the side seam, turning under $\frac{1}{2}''$ (1.3cm). In a minute you will sew over them with your bias finish.

Note: I know this sewing order is not correct for tailored garments. Experienced sewers may want to sew the sleeve seam and side seam and then set in the sleeve. In that case add the finishing strip on the first sleeve sewing or add it in a second sewing (as previously noted), but do not begin and end the seam of the finishing strip at the underarm seam. Start and stop the finishing strip over to the side of the underarm seam so this seam won't be so bulky.

The sewing order I first describe is easier for students handling the bulk of the quilted fabrics.

Hint: Recently I have been doubling the straight strip used as a seam finish, cutting them 2-$\frac{1}{2}''$ (6.3cm) wide, folding them in half wrong sides together, and pressing them. This results in a neater inside seam finish, and it is easier to do the hand sewing. It's never too late to learn new tricks.

Inside Patch Pockets

Cut one or two 14″ × 7-$\frac{1}{2}''$ (35cm × 19cm) rectangles of lining fabric. Fold each in half, right sides together. Sew side seams. Clip, turn right side out, and press. Pin in place on inside fronts on the lining, allowing the bottom pocket edge to fall into the bottom seam. The bottom edge will be finished with the bias later. Hand-sew side pocket seams in place to the lining, just catching the lining fabric. See Fig. 2-12. You can place patch pockets on the outside if you are willing to duplicate your quilting design to make the pocket flow with the design. I have sewn pockets in the side seams, but then the jacket is not reversible. My customers always want pockets, so I usually put them on the inside.

Collar

A collar can be added at this point. Staystitch the neck edge. Clip to the staystitching. Cut two collar pieces of outer shell fabric. Place one collar piece right sides together with the jacket neckline. Pin. Place the other collar piece with its right side to wrong side of the jacket lining. See Fig. 2-13. Sew the neck seam. Bring both collar pieces up in place. Add a piece of batting in between the collar pieces, pin, and draw part of your design on the collar. Machine quilt. The outside edge of the collar will be finished with bias at a later step. This method is not your usual way to make a collar. Remember, the jacket also looks good without a collar.

Closures

If you want buttons and loops or ties for your jacket, add them now. See Fig. 2-14. For loops, cut a bias strip 1-$\frac{1}{4}''$ (3.1cm) with enough length for the number of loops needed at 3″ (7.5cm) each. Fold the strip in half lengthwise with the right sides together. Stitch $\frac{1}{4}''$ (6mm) from the raw

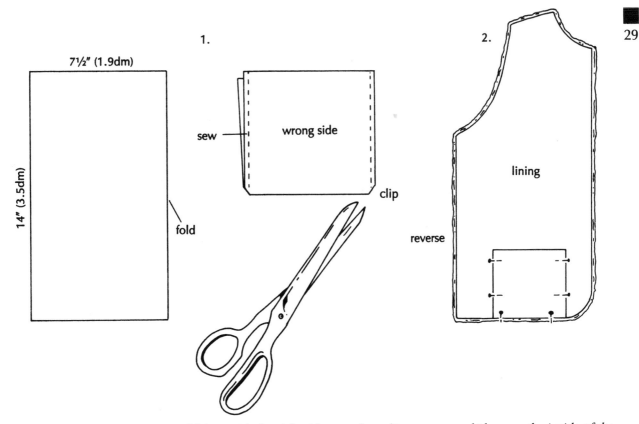

Fig. 2-12. Pockets. 1. Fold strip of fabric with the right sides together, clip, reverse, and place on the inside of the jacket front. 2. You now are ready to hand-sew the sides of the pocket to the lining. The bottom of the pocket is attached when the outside bias is attached.

edges. Turn right-side-out with the loop turner or a safety pin. Press as shown in Fig. 2-14, part 1. Pin in place on the jacket right front with the raw edges even with the raw edges of the jacket.

See Fig. 2-14, part 3. Loops are sewn later as you add the bias finish.

Ties are formed like the loops except they are longer (7″ [17.5cm] is good). See Fig. 2-14,

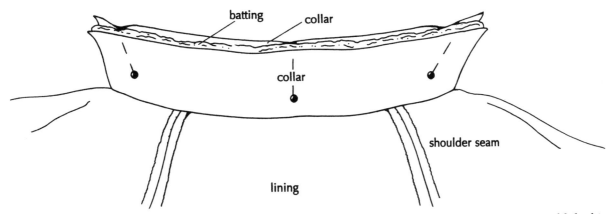

Fig. 2-13. Attaching the collar to the jacket. The two collar pieces are not sewn together until you add the bias binding. Round the front edges of the collar.

EASY QUILTED JACKET MADE FROM ONE FABRIC

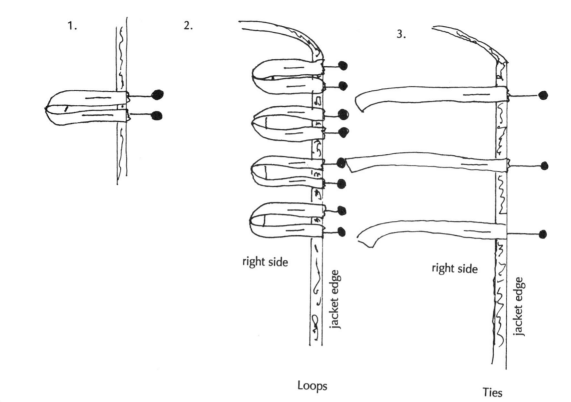

Loops

Ties

Fig. 2-14. *Loops and ties. 1. Shape to form the loop with pressing. 2. With placement of the multiple loops, notice the alignment of the raw edges, and space the loops evenly. 3. Ties pinned to the right side of the jacket are ready to be sewn when the bias edging is sewn.*

part 3. Buttons and buttonholes are added after the jacket is finished. See Chapter 5 sections on the Koss Method of Appliqué and cording for more discussion of working with bias and cording.

Note: The automatic buttonhole maker on my computer machine will not handle the buttonholes on a jacket if I try to make them after the bias trim is attached. The bias interferes with the completely flat area needed for the seeing eye of the buttonhole maker. Instead, I use the semiautomatic buttonhole maker.

Bias Finish

You can make the color of your bias outside trim the same color as your jacket. Many of our figures are not complemented by a straight line of contrasting color around the hips. Cut bias 2-$\frac{1}{2}$" (6.3cm) wide using a rotary cutter and mat.

See Fig. 2-15 and Chapter 1 for cutting and piecing bias. Instructions are for a double French bias.

With napped fabrics, lay your strips out on the worktable and check for direction of light and dark. Piece if necessary. Fold bias in half the long way, wrong sides together, and press (Fig. 2-15, part 4). It takes about 3-$\frac{1}{2}$ yds. (3.2m) of bias to finish the edges and sleeves of the jacket.

The finishing edges can be cut on the straight of your fabric the same size as bias. The neckline would have to be bias but straight strips can be used in the remainder of the jacket if you do not round your edges. Straight strips will not go around curves. The bottom corners will then need a miter (see Fig. 2-16).

Note: I never use commercial bias. It is made of inexpensive fabric that doesn't always match and needs to be preshrunk—a mess to do. In addition, bias directions usually indicate mak-

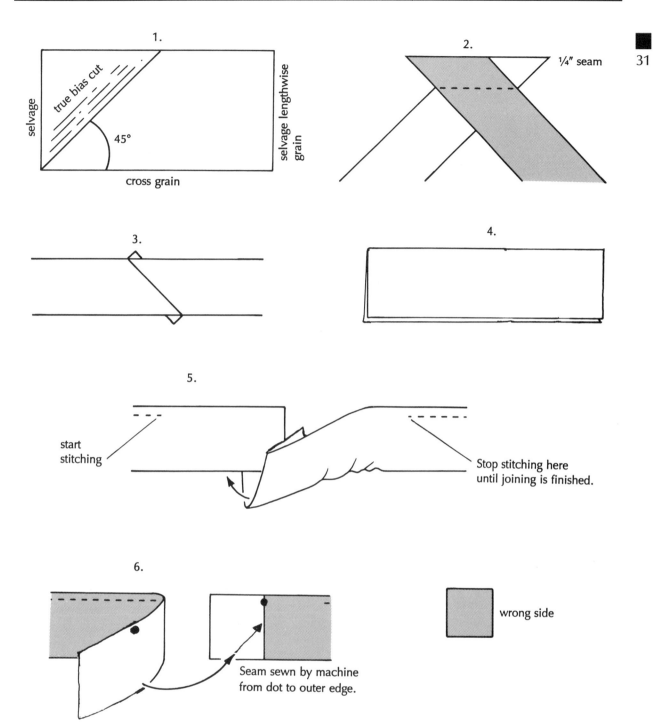

Fig. 2-15. *Cutting and piecing bias. 1. True bias. 2. Piecing bias. 3. Finished seam of pieced bias. 4. Fold and press the bias for double French bias. 5. Fold one edge of the bias to the inside and lap it over the other bias end to finish the bias edge. 6. The second method to finish bias edges. Mark a dot where bias will join. Seam and then press the seam open with your fingers, pin it to the jacket edge and finish machine stitching.*

EASY QUILTED JACKET MADE FROM ONE FABRIC

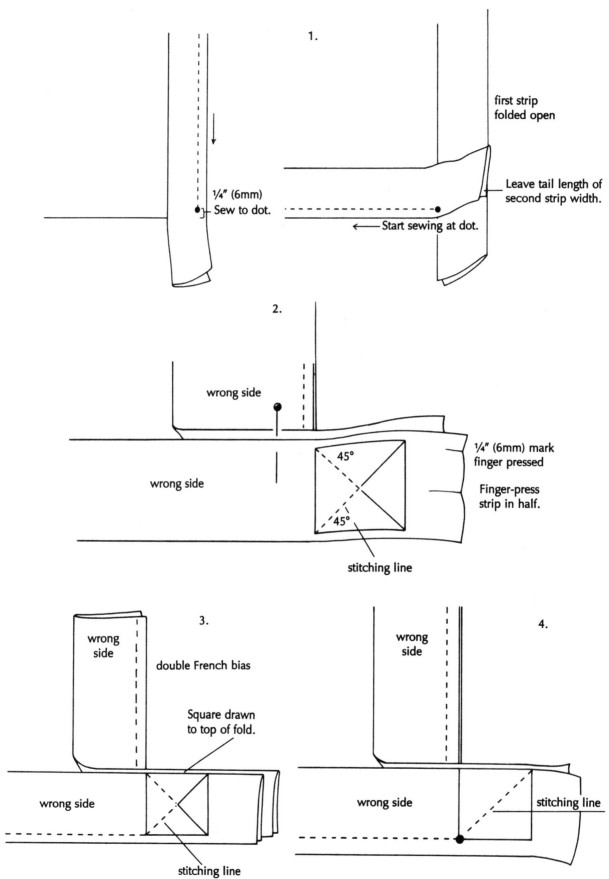

1.

first strip
folded open

¼" (6mm)
• Sew to dot.

Leave tail length of
second strip width.

← Start sewing at dot.

2.

wrong side

wrong side

¼" (6mm) mark
finger pressed

Finger-press
strip in half.

45°

45°

stitching line

3.

wrong
side

double French bias

Square drawn
to top of fold.

wrong side

stitching line

4.

wrong
side

wrong side

stitching line

ing continuous bias, which I never do. I have not found the idea easy for students to execute.

Sewing Bias to Jacket

Starting at the bottom of the jacket near the side seam (but not on the side seam), sew the right side of the bias to the right side of the top edge in a $\frac{1}{4}''$ (6mm) seam or slightly larger to be sure of catching all edges. See Fig. 2-17. Continue sewing all around the jacket in one long seam, clipping bias as you round bottom front edges and collar.

There are two ways to join your bias edges. For both methods leave first and last 3" (7.5cm) unstitched to give you room to position the fabric. The first method is to fold under one short raw edge and lap the other end under the folded edge. See Fig. 2-15. Pin and finish sewing jacket edge.

The second method is to place a dot at the exact point on each end of the bias where they will meet. Remove jacket from the machine, lap the two ends of bias right sides together matching the dots. Pin. Stitch a $\frac{1}{4}''$ (6mm) seam in the bias. Finger-press seam open. Line up on the jacket and complete stitching the bias to the jacket edge. See Fig. 2-15. Repeat with the sleeves.

Bring bias to the inside and hand-stitch in place. The hand work of finishing the bias and

inside seams takes about four hours and is good to do at night while watching television. If you have trouble getting the finishing strips smooth in the armhole area, put the inside-out sleeve on your knee to form the seam. I call my hand stitch an appliqué stitch. (It's also called a fell stitch.) See Fig. 2-18. I use the shortest quilting needle I can thread. The shorter the needle, the shorter the distance your hand needs to go back. Leave the knot under the fold, come straight down into the jacket, and take a short bite when coming up to the bias again in one step. Come straight down again and repeat. I take three or four stitches before pulling the thread through. You may want to wear a thimble to avoid injuring your finger.

Mitering

If you have square corners, now is a good time to practice mitering. See illustrations of three different miters in Fig. 2-16, parts 2-4. Make a sample of the three miters and keep them handy. All you need is a little understanding of the square and you can do it.

For all three miters, you will sew the strips to the jacket the same way. Mark the corner with a dot $\frac{1}{4}''$ (6mm) from both edges for the seam allowance. Sew the first side strip, with a $\frac{1}{4}''$ seam allowance, to the dot. Stop and backstitch. Take

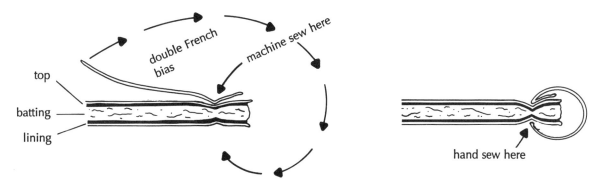

Fig. 2-17. *Sewing bias binding to the garment edge. Raw edges of bias are aligned with the jacket's raw edges.*

Fig. 2-16. *1. Stitching strips ready for miter. Stitching of edging for all three miters. 2. Miter for single-layer bias (or straight-edge strip) drawing the square to find the stitching line. Finger-press the strip in half. 3. Drawing the square to find the stitching line for double French bias (or straight-edge strip doubled). 4. Drawing the square to find the stitching line for flat straps (sashing).*

EASY QUILTED JACKET MADE FROM ONE FABRIC

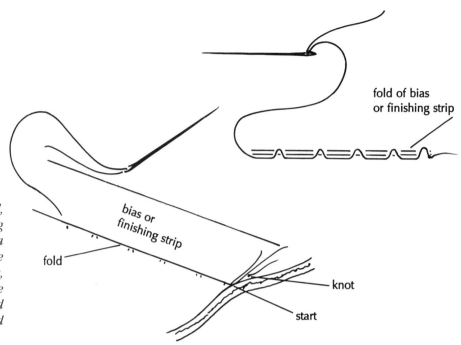

fold of bias
or finishing strip

bias or
finishing strip

fold

knot

start

Fig. 2-18. *Hand stitching, fell, or appliqué stitch. Working from right to left, pick up a thread on the top fold, come down to the bottom fabric, take a $\frac{1}{4}''$ (6mm) bit and come straight up to the top fold again. After practice, hand stitching is relaxing.*

your work out of the machine. Open out the first bias strip and pin it in place. Cut strip and leave an overhang the same width as the folded-out strip on which you will make the miter. Position second strip to start at the outside edge of the first opened strip. Find the dot and mark on the second strip (Fig. 2-16, part 1). Put the needle in the fabric a few stitches forward from the dot and backstitch to the dot. Then continue sewing seam forward. Both strip seams stop exactly at the dot, not behind or beyond the dot. Flip last sewn strip out and finger-press. Then turn garment over. All three miters are started in this manner.

1. *Miter for single-layer bias or straight fabric finish.* Working with the wrong side of one strip corner, finger-press strip in half the long way. Open out. This marks the center. Finger-press $\frac{1}{4}''$ (6mm) seam allowance or measurement of your seam allowance on both sides of strip. See Fig. 2-16, part 2. Mark and measure the line from the stitching corner to the outer seam allowance. Using this measurement, mark a square between seam allowances. Draw diagonal lines from corners of the square. Check with your see-through ruler to be sure the tri-

angles formed are 45-degree corners. Position right sides of both strip corners on top of each other with the marking on top. Pin. Sew right-angle lines shown by triangular stitching line in Fig. 2-16, part 2, backstitching at both ends of stitching and sewing a single stitch straight across the point of the triangle. It's easier to sew from the outside edge to the dot. Trim and reverse to right side.

2. *Miter for double French bias or double straight strip.* Draw a square to get your 45-degree angle as you did in single bias, only this time draw to the fold (see Fig. 2-16, part 3). You use just the bottom seam allowance. Finish as previously noted.

3. *Miter for flat strips.* This miter is used in your piecing and is sewn on what quilters call sashing. Again, draw a square to the top edge and disregard the top seam allowance (see Fig. 2-16, part 4). Your stitching line is the diagonal line formed from the dot to the outer edge. Trim seam and press open.

The benefits of using double French bias where you can are ease in hand sewing and longer wear of the doubled fabric. The edges of clothing and bindings of quilts take the brunt of the wear. Some books advocate doing the final stitching by machine. I never have been able to do this neatly, so I stitch by hand.

Another option with your bias outside trim is to pull it all to the inside if you don't want the color or a line interfering with your jacket design.

You now have mastered the basic quilted jacket. You're ready to try a pieced jacket finished like the one-fabric jacket or to jump to the dense-quilted jacket (Chapter 6), which is finished a little differently. Stop a few minutes to clean and oil your machine and put in a new needle. Machines deserve tender loving care.

PART II
■ ■ ■
MAKING PIECED JACKETS AND COATS

In this section you will learn to make a one-of-a-kind jacket or coat using smaller pieces to form the fabric. This process is called piecing. There are many ways to give that fabric interest, texture, and character. I will show you my favorite techniques. In Chapter 3, making a Seminole Indian patchwork coat is explained in detail. If you don't care to make this coat, study the directions anyway, because many techniques are explained here that I later will assume you know. Other piecing methods use the same basic construction as the coat. In fact, you already know how to quilt and put together these garments. They are finished just like the jacket made from one fabric. In constructing this coat and all pieced garments, a fabric is cut from your pattern to become your palette for decoration. This fabric is called "backing." Some designers piece directly on batting or lighter fleece, but I prefer using backing and add batting later.

CHAPTER 3

■ ■ ■

Seminole Indian Patchwork Coat

Since the coat in this chapter uses Seminole Indian patchwork, we will begin with Seminole instructions. The first part contains general instructions for making Seminole patterns and the next section provides illustrations and instructions for specific designs.

Seminole Indian patchwork consists of strips of fabric sewn together by machine. These sewn strips (strata) are recut into sections (segments) and resewn in different ways to arrive at any number of pieced bands. The design variations are limitless. See Figs. 3-1 and 3-3.

The Seminole Indians of Florida started the designs when missionaries introduced hand-turned sewing machines and cloth in the late 1800s. The Indians used the bands to decorate clothing for the women, men, and children. Fine examples still can be found today. Their ingenuity has enriched the quilting tradition. Seminole Indian patchwork is a version of strip quilting and as such fits in well with the desire today to make attractive quilting faster than by hand methods.

If you are familiar with sewing the patchwork, skip to Making the Seminole Indian Patchwork for a coat (on page 53). However, note the changes from the usual way of making Seminole necessary to obtain sheen in the coat and the necessity to enlarge the blocks when working with a heavier fabric.

■ General Directions

See Fig. 3-4 for illustration of the terms used in Seminole.

Art Nouveau flower.

Fig. 3-1. *Man's Seminole Indian patchwork jacket. Cotton-polyester corduroy with cotton lining. Seminole designs include chevron, Design #1, and two-band triangle. Machine-quilted with even-feed foot, using some geometric templates and the remainder of the machine quilting following the design ¼" (6mm) away from the edge. 1985. Owner: Marvin Spencer.*

Choose fabrics of compatible weight and composition; 100-percent cotton works best. The Indians used only solids, but you can use prints as long as there is enough contrast in your choice. Choosing a print and several solids to match makes color choice easier. Preshrink all fabrics and trims. Press.

Find the straight of the fabric by pulling a thread or ripping the end. Fold the fabric once in half, selvage to selvage, then in half again with the top edges even. Press and pay particular attention to flatten the side folds so you won't have a bow when your strips are cut. You now have

one piece of fabric ready to cut into strips with the rotary cutter. Repeat with each fabric used in your design.

Hint: Leave your fabrics folded until the project is finished. You are ready at any time to cut a needed strip.

To cut the strips, arrange your fabric on the mat for the rotary cutter so that you can cut without crossing your arms. The rotary cutter is great if it is used safely. Cut against a heavy Plexiglas ruler. Keep your scissors with you to cut little

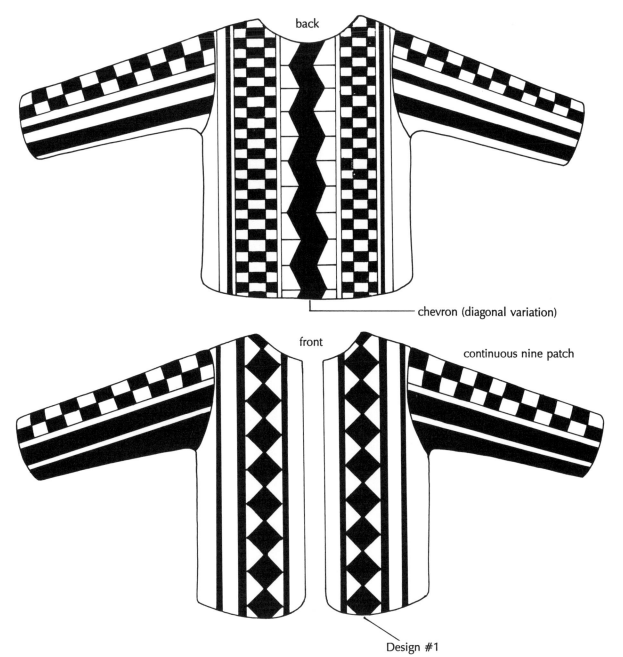

back

chevron (diagonal variation)

front

continuous nine patch

Design #1

Fig. 3-2. *Seminole Indian patchwork designs for a coat. The directions in the text are for Seminole Design #1, continuous nine patch, and diagonal sewn as a chevron.*

places the rotary cutter misses. If you try to line up the fabric again and recut, a mess results. See Fig. 3-5 for rotary cutter layout.

Use $\frac{1}{4}''$ (6mm) seams throughout. Mark your sewing machine bed $\frac{1}{4}''$ (6mm) from the needle with masking tape if your presser foot is not $\frac{1}{4}''$ (6mm). Machines with different needle positions

will give you a $\frac{1}{4}''$ (6mm) seam by moving the needle position. Press the band from the back with seams going in one direction. Press from the front and make sure the strip is pulled to its fullest width. The sewing of the strips into strata is a good place to use your serger using a $\frac{1}{4}''$ (6mm) seam allowance consistently. The second stage of

Fig. 3-3. *Seminole skirt featuring bright colors and lots of rickrack made of 100-percent cotton. I received it in trade in New Mexico, and suspect it is of Indian origin.*

the sewing is best done on the regular machine so you carefully can match seams.

Mark and cut strata according to specific directions for the design you are making.

Sew segments into bands according to your pattern. It's important here to talk to yourself. Lay a portion of the design out on the work table and find a sewing sequence. It works best to have the

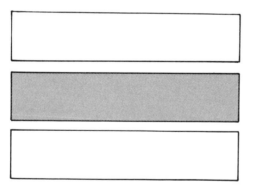

strips

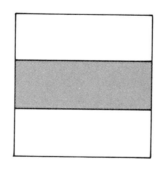

strata

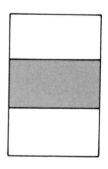

segment

Fig. 3-4. *Seminole Indian patchwork terms: strips, strata, and segments for the Seminole coat.*

MAKING PIECED JACKETS AND COATS

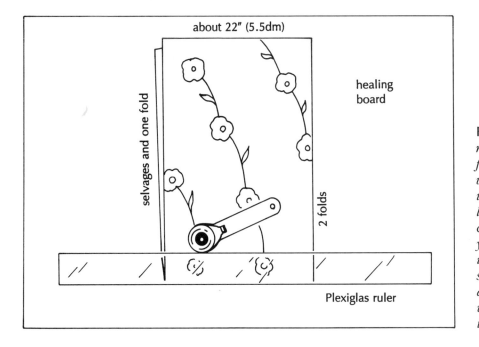

about 22″ (5.5dm)

selvages and one fold

healing board

2 folds

Plexiglas ruler

Fig. 3-5. *Rotary cutter for a right-handed sewer. Fabric is folded twice, selvage to selvage. If the rotary cutter is used properly, it is the biggest labor saver and tool for accuracy available in recent years. I started making Seminole by cutting strips with scissors that were not straight and then tried ripping, which was a mess and distorted threads of dark fabrics.*

seam allowances going in the same direction (down) on most designs. Look at how each pair goes together and do each pair the same way. See Fig. 3-6 and find a sewing sequence for segments. This prevents your design from going in two directions. Each design has a special trick in order to get it together easily. Sew pairs together and do not cut the thread between. Cut pairs apart and sew in fours, eights, etc. until you have completed your band.

Press the band from the back first, with seams all going in one direction. Notice the bias ten-

dency in the band, and get the band as straight as possible. Light spraying with spray starch helps flatten and straighten the band. You may use your rotary cutter to cut off the v's, but be sure to leave $\frac{1}{4}″$ (6mm) seam allowance between the fabric edge and the point of the first design. See Fig. 3-7 for finding cutting and sewing lines.

Next, sew straight strips on the sides of your Seminole design bands. Vary the width of the side strips between $\frac{3}{4}″$ (2cm) and $2\text{-}\frac{1}{2}″$ (7.5cm). It helps to sew side strips from the back (side strip on bottom wrong-side-down then the design band

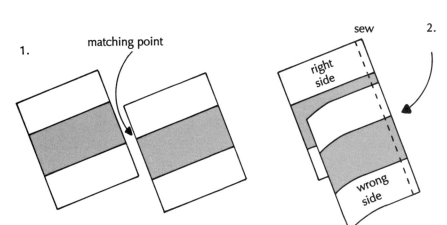

1. matching point

sew   2.

right side

wrong side

Fig. 3-6. *Finding a sewing sequence for segments. Understanding and seeing matching points makes your sewing faster and more accurate. Remember to sew all your pairs without cutting the thread in between; then sew fours, eights, and so forth. 1. Match bottom line of the stripe in the first segment to the top line of the second. 2. Sew each pair the same way. Match with the bottom of the strip.*

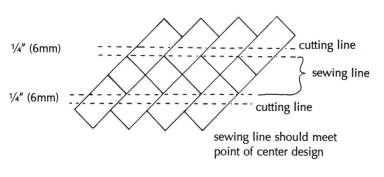

Fig. 3-7. *Seminole cutting and sewing lines. Your see-through ruler and rotary cutter help here. To make your band straight, you sometimes may have to rip out a piece or two that don't match well. Sometimes the problem is in the pressing. Sewing with cotton, I do not always cut off the v's.*

1/4" (6mm)

1/4" (6mm)

cutting line

sewing line

cutting line

sewing line should meet point of center design

right-side-down against the side strip). This makes matching points on the band easier. You may sew the side strips on before adding Seminole to the garment or pin the Seminole strip to the garment and then sew the side strips.

It's difficult to give exact amounts of fabric needed for each band. Patterns cut on an angle take more fabric. The length of the band given for each pattern is based on one 45" (1.2m) width of each strip.

When sewing a $\frac{3}{4}$" (2cm) strip to another strip, be very careful of the seam allowance when sewing the first row. To sew the second row, position your work so the $\frac{3}{4}$" (2cm) strip is on top and the bulk is to your right. If your machine has a $\frac{1}{4}$" (6mm) presser foot, you can sew following the right side of the presser foot along the sewn row.

If your presser foot is wider, eyeball your stitching and have confidence that you will find the place to sew, and eyeball your stitching. If your machine has the capacity to change needle positions, you can move the needle and get your $\frac{1}{4}$" (6mm) seam allowance. See Fig. 3-8 on sewing in a $\frac{3}{4}$" (2cm) seam that will be straight.

A word of caution when making multiple-strip strata is necessary. Alternate the direction of sewing the strips together. Sewing many rows from the same direction will give your finished band a bow. Tips like this are based on my mistakes.

You can easily vary the dimensions of your bands as long as you remember to have an extra $\frac{1}{4}$" (6mm) on the outside pieces to attach to a strip. Doubling and tripling a pattern, especially the square-type bands, allows for quick and easy quilt

blocks. I will be showing you some of this in the sections on quilt blocks and skirt making. The band-type designs are good borders for quilts and other household furnishings.

Your finished bands are completed with angled ends. To straighten the ends for ease in use, do the following: Cut the band anywhere in the middle with a straight cut (you might want to cut in place where the match is not so swift). Bring

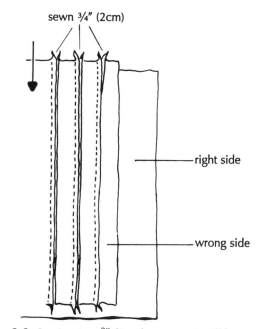

sewn 3/4" (2cm)

right side

wrong side

Fig. 3-8. *Sewing in a $\frac{3}{4}$" (2cm) seam so it will be straight. Practice this technique. Begin sewing at the arrow and follow previously sewn line with the presser foot. If the narrow lines are wavy, the piece looks poor. Multiple narrow lines done correctly are a great design look.*

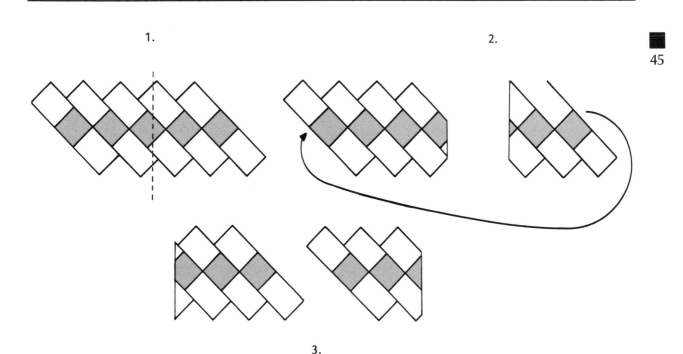

1.   2.

3.

Fig. 3-9. *Straightening ends of a Seminole band. Do this to have a straight edge and not waste even a small amount of your piecing. Watch where you cut in multiple strata bands so the ends will continue the design. Step 1: Cut in the center. Step 2: Bring ends around, continuing the pattern. Step 3: Sew matching pattern.*

the ends around to meet following the pattern. Sew. See Fig. 3-9 for an illustration of straightening the ends of a Seminole band.

It is possible to make a Seminole curve for around a gored skirt. See *E-Z Does It* by Edith Zimmer, 7776 Golfcrest Drive, San Diego, CA 92119-1983.

From Fig. 3-15 on square designs and setting them on the diagonal, you learn a nifty way to set all squares on point and make a band. The results are a bias seam on the triangle between the blocks. This seam needs special handling. First, check your completed band with your see-through ruler and trim. Remember to leave $\frac{1}{4}''$ (6mm) above the point for seam allowance. When adding this band to clothing or strips, it's very easy to stretch the bias seam. In *Speed-Cut Quilts* (listed in the Bibliography), Donna Poster gives some of the best advice I've read about working with bias:

When sewing a bias edge to a straight edge, try to sew with the bias piece on the bottom. If it's on top, your machine foot will stretch it by pushing the fabric ahead. When pressing a bias piece with a bias edge, either set the iron down and pick it up without moving it or gently move the iron with the grain of the bias piece. If you've pre-washed a fabric that will be cut into triangles, diamonds, or other bias shapes, use a spray-on fabric sizing when ironing it.

Figs. 3-10 through 3-16 are illustrations of specific Seminole designs.

In Fig. 3-10, Design #1 shows the most frequently used and shown band of the Seminole patterns. It can be varied by adding multiple rows in the center, using three colors instead of two, or using three colors reversed every other row.

Step 1: Make strata, sew and press. Step 2: Cut $1\text{-}\frac{1}{4}''$ (3.1cm). Match top inside strip to bottom of next strip (at arrow). Step 3: Resew.

You will have a band 36" (0.9m) long when finished.

Fig. 3-11 shows adding side strips to segments. Basically it is Design #1, but the band is

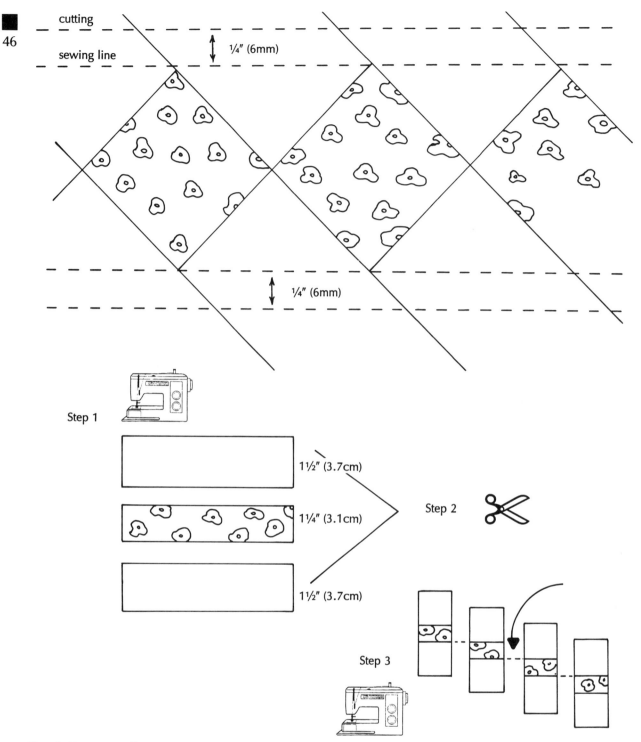

Fig. 3-10. *Design #1.*

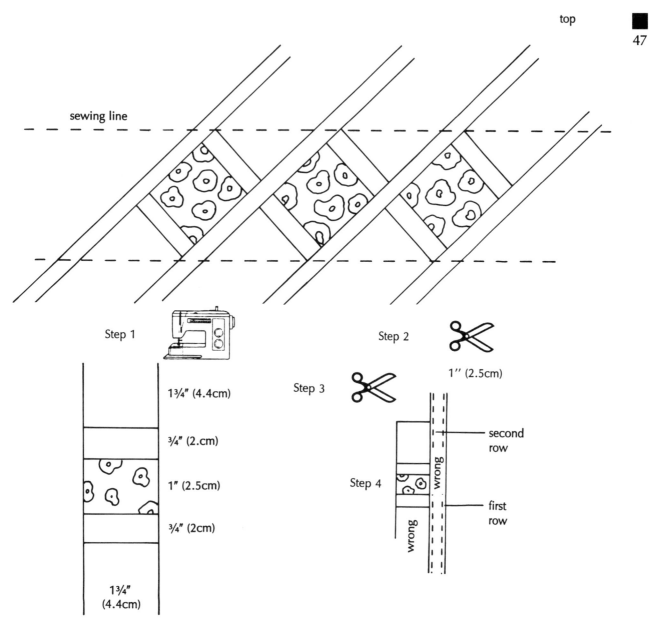

Fig. 3-11. *Adding side strips to segments.*

lengthened and the middle square is made to look like it is surrounded with a color. Many of the other designs can have side bands added.

Step 1: Cut strips. Sew strata and press. Step 2: Cut stratas into 1″ (2.5cm) segments. Step 3: Cut extra ¾″ (2cm) lengths of dark color. Sew segments to dark lengths without overlapping segments. Step 4: Press segment/band assembly open and press seam allowance to the segment. Cut segments apart. Step 5: Assemble as shown in the illustration. Find your matching point.

Note: When sewing in ¾″ (2cm) strips, first sew one side. To sew the second side, have ¾″

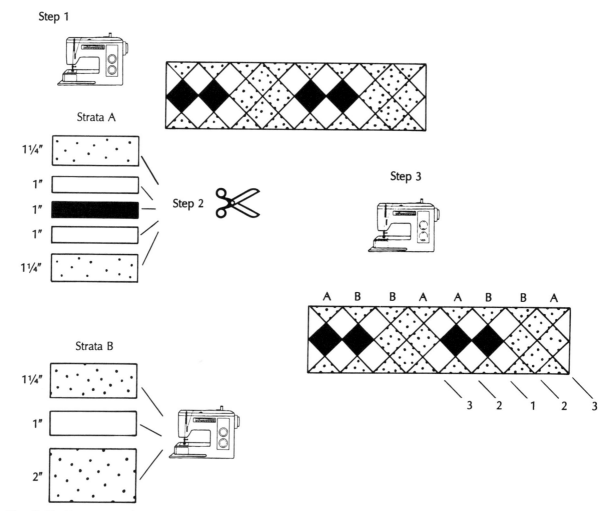

Fig. 3-12. *Two-strata design.*

(2cm) strip on top. Use $\frac{1}{4}''$ (6mm) presser foot as a guide or eyeball it to make $\frac{1}{4}''$ (6mm) in the center of the strip.

Finished band is 40″ (1m) long.

Fig. 3-12 features a two-strata design. Learn to sew two strata and combine them into a band. In order not to confuse yourself, lay strips on your worktable in the order you want to sew them.

Step 1: Cut two separate strata. Sew and press. Step 2: Cut each band 1″ (2.5cm) straight. Step 3: Follow sewing sequence. Assemble all seam #1s first. Assemble seam #2s next and reverse the

segments. Now you have one design unit. Lay out and connect the design unit last (seam #3s). This is very logical and not as difficult as it looks.

Finished band is 63″ (1.6m) long.

Fig. 3-13's diagonal designs take more fabric but have a great look. I use the chevron or mirror image more than the first diagonal design. Avoid confusion by reading the directions carefully concerning folding the strata and cutting so the segments are ready for the sewing machine.

Step 1: Cut strips. Sew and press. Step 2: Draw and cut a 45-degree angle, cut segments 2″ (5cm). Step 3: Reassemble.

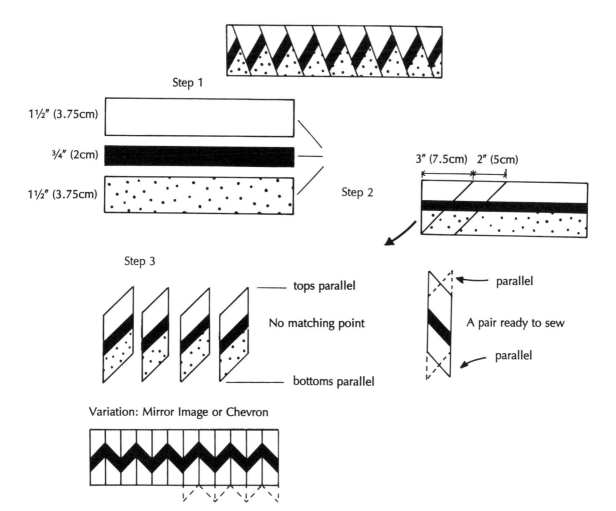

Step 1

1½″ (3.75cm)

¾″ (2cm)

1½″ (3.75cm)

Step 2

3″ (7.5cm) 2″ (5cm)

Step 3

tops parallel

No matching point

bottoms parallel

parallel

A pair ready to sew

parallel

Variation: Mirror Image or Chevron

Fig. 3-13. *Diagonal designs.*

For the mirror image or chevron variation, make two bands as in the previous directions. Place the two bands right sides together and align them exactly. Establish a 45-degree angle. Cut away. Cut segments and maintain the angle. Leave pairs together to sew. Start sewing each set of pairs on the low side or high side—not both. It still is best to have seams go down as you sew.

Finished band is 18″ (.4m) long.

More variations are multicolored outside strips that are wider, reverse segments, or adding plain strips between segments or groups of segments.

Nine patch or checkerboard (Fig. 3-14) is a design you will use frequently if you are a quilter. People will ask if you put all those little squares together, and you will nod yes.

Step 1: Cut strips. Step 2: Sew strata and press. Step 3: Cut strata into 1″ (2.5cm) segments. Step 4: Choose an assembly method.

Hint: Be very careful in measuring and matching when setting straight pieces together. Nine patch is a two-strata design. Start thinking of designs with multiple strata (A, B, C, B, A, etc.). An example is the reverse A's shown at the right.

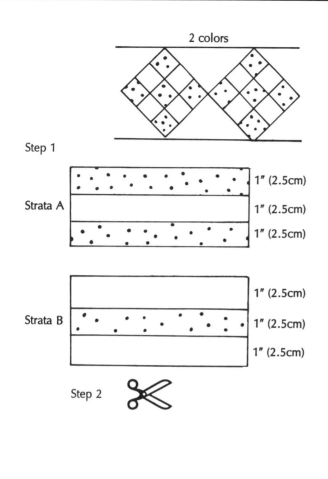

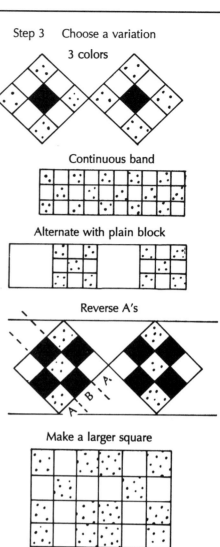

Fig. 3-14. *Nine patch or checkerboard.*

The top design is 94″ (2.6m) long.

Fig. 3-15 features a square design set on point. This is very effective and the results give you much yardage. See Lassie Whittman's work (listed in the Bibliography) to see how she further complicates this design by adding borders all around the square in log cabin piecing fashion.

Step 1: Cut and sew three strata as shown.

Hint: Lay them out on a table in order of sewing to keep from mixing and confusing them.

Step 2: Cut strata A 1-¼″ (3.1cm) and cut strata B and C ¾″ (2cm). Step 3: Assemble like the illustration, leaving each unit separate. Do not join the units. Step 4: To make triangles or set squares on point, cut a strip of medium-color fabric 2-¾″ (6.8cm) wide and cut into 4-½″ (1.1dm) pieces. Step 5: Sew one plain strip to one design unit and continue until you have a long band alternating plain and design blocks. Step 6: Cut on a diagonal through the plain block, all cuts in the same direction, and leave a ½″ (1.3cm) seam. Step 7: Sew as at top of the illustration.

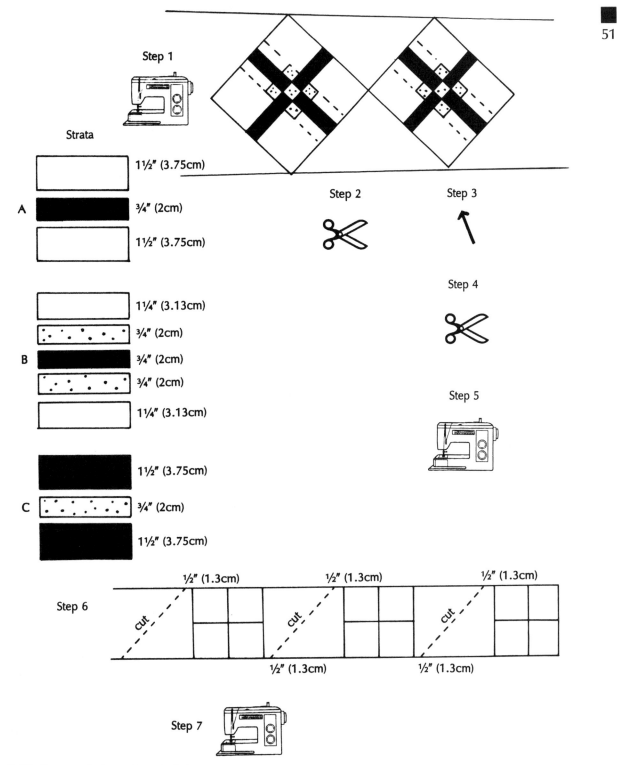

Step 1

Strata

1½" (3.75cm)

A   ¾" (2cm)

1½" (3.75cm)

Step 2

Step 3

Step 4

Step 5

1¼" (3.13cm)

¾" (2cm)

B   ¾" (2cm)

¾" (2cm)

1¼" (3.13cm)

1½" (3.75cm)

C   ¾" (2cm)

1½" (3.75cm)

½" (1.3cm)   ½" (1.3cm)   ½" (1.3cm)

Step 6   cut   cut   cut

½" (1.3cm)   ½" (1.3cm)

Step 7

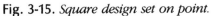

Fig. 3-15. *Square design set on point.*

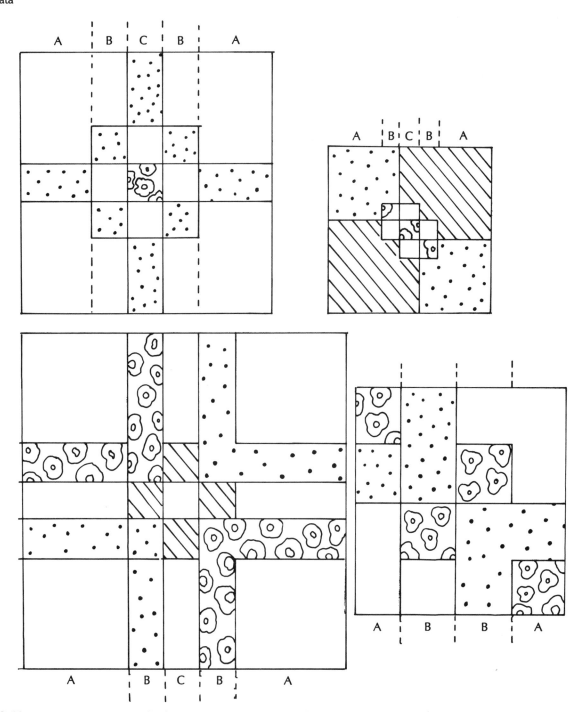

Fig. 3-16. *More square Seminole designs. Now you are ready to get your graph paper and design your own squares. Each graph paper block equals ½" (1.3cm). Add seam allowance.*

Hint: Use this method to join any square blocks.

Finished band is 53″ (1.5m) long.

■ Making the Coat

The subtle light change in this coat makes it a smart, practical garment to wear. You will get compliments and smiles wearing the coat in the grocery store or wherever you are. It's easy to change the directions and make the coat a jacket if you prefer. Dimensions for a jacket will be in parentheses or brackets. See the color section for examples of finished pieces.

In order to construct this jacket, you need experience in putting together Seminole Indian patchwork. I suggest practicing the three designs used in the coat in 100-percent cotton in the smaller sizes given in the Seminole instructions. Two rules for Seminole construction are broken when making the coat. The first is the use of polyester/cotton fabric, which is used for the added sheen of the blended fabric. The second is ripping the strips of corduroy on the length of the grain to create the difference in the nap that gives this coat its beauty. The Seminole pattern in the coat is enlarged because of the corduroy's heaviness.

Shopping List

The shopping list for this coat is the same as the list for the plain jacket except for the amounts of fabric (see the Chapter 2 Shopping List).

☐ 8 yds. (7.2m) of corduroy (5 yds. [4.5m] for jacket) in a medium to dark color. Polyester in the fabric increases the contrast or sheen, as you can see when comparing cotton corduroy to the blends. While at the store, turn some of the nap and place it against the opposite direction to be sure of sufficient contrast.

☐ 5 yds. (4.5m) of lining fabric (3 yds. [2.7m] for jacket).

☐ 1 yd. (0.9m) corduroy fabric for bias trim, usually the same color as the outer coat.

☐ A rotary cutter, mat, and Plexiglas ruler for cutting the Seminole Indian patchwork.

☐ 6 yds. (5.4m) (3 yds. [2.7m] for jacket) of an old, prewashed material as a backing fabric. Old sheets, cheap fabric from an outlet, or a fabric you'll never use elsewhere are all handy. (Start a pile of such fabrics.) In this coat the color of the backing does not have to be white, as it will later when you must work with white or off-white. This is a good place to use that print you don't know why you bought.

Caution: Never try to hand-quilt on fine percale. It's too dense, but you can machine quilt it.

■ Seminole Indian Patchwork

Review basic directions in Chapter 2, and see Figs. 3-2, 3-17, and 3-18 for Seminole Indian patchwork designs used on the coat.

First, rip the strips in the numbers and widths indicated for each design. Rip on the length of the grain, an exception to the usual way of doing Seminole. The length of the grain gives you the contrast and ripping makes the pieces straight on a rib (and yes, it makes a mess). See Figs. 3-17 and 3-18 for the Seminole designs.

Next, lay the strips out on your work table, separating each design. Reverse the nap of the center strips. Your layout should look like the sewn stratas on the drawing. Look at your designs from the side to check that you have reversed the nap. You can feel the difference in the direction of the nap by rubbing your hand against the fabric.

Sew strips together on a serger (if you have one) or use the even-feed foot on your regular machine with $\frac{1}{4}$″ (6mm) seams.

Press seams in one direction from the back. Flip to the front. Press, making sure to have the full width pulled flat.

Chevron design–variation of diagonal
(see Fig. 3-13)

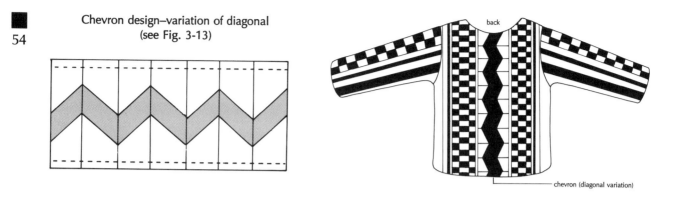

chevron (diagonal variation)

Sewn strata

2" (5cm)

45°

cut away

3" × 90" (60") [7.5cm × 1.6m (1.5m)]

2" × 90" (60") [5cm × 1.6m (1.5m)]

3" × 90" (60") [7.5cm × 1.6m (1.5m)]

Nine patch in continuous band
(see Fig. 3-14)

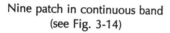

Two-strata sewn

2½" (6.2cm)

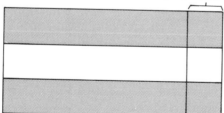

2½" × 130" (90") [6.2cm × 3.6m (2.5m)]

2½" × 130" (90") [6.2cm × 3.6m (2.5m)]

2½" × 130" (90") [6.2cm × 3.6m (2.5m)]

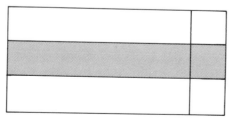

2½" × 130" (90") [6.2cm × 3.6m (2.5m)]

2½" × 130" (90") [6.2cm × 3.6m (2.5m)]

2½" × 130" (90") [6.2cm × 3.6m (2.5m)]

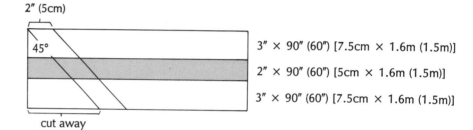

MAKING PIECED JACKETS AND COATS

Design #1 (see Fig. 3-10)
finished design

sewing line

front

continuous nine patch

Design #1

sewn strata

cut
3″ (7.5cm)

$3\frac{1}{2}'' \times 135''$ (96″) [8.7cm $\times$ 3.7m (2.6m)]

$3'' \times 135''$ (96″) [7.5cm $\times$ 3.7m (2.6m)]

$3\frac{1}{2}'' \times 135''$ (96″) [8.7cm $\times$ 3.7m (2.6m)]

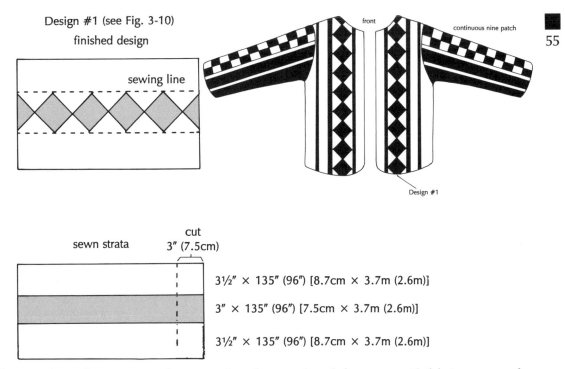

Figs. 3-17 and 3-18. *Chart of cutting strips for Seminole Indian patchwork for a coat with fabric amounts for a jacket in parentheses. It is always wise to buy extra fabric.*

Cut with rotary cutter in the dimensions given in the drawing.

Lay out your design, find your sewing order, and resew. Here the sewing machine works better for me than the serger. It's easier to see matching seams. Refer to the General Directions earlier in this chapter for tricks in putting together each band.

Press bands using lots of steam or your water squirt bottle. Some pressing must be done on the front of the fabric. This will distort the nap. Later you can brush the fabric to return the nap.

Cut the v-shaped pieces of fabric (see Fig. 3-7) from the Seminole leaving $\frac{1}{4}''$ (6mm) seam allowance. Notice that the seam allowance on the chevron design is not at the point of the inside strip. Move your seam allowance to the sides as much as you can.

You now have your Seminole ready to piece to your backing fabric.

■ Assembling the Outer Shell

Cut your five pattern pieces from the backing fabric, allowing an extra $\frac{1}{2}''$ (1.3cm) all around. Lay out the backing pieces on your work table, being sure to reverse one front and one sleeve.

Start by pinning the chevron design strip on the center back in the exact middle. Pin all the way down.

From your remaining corduroy rip two strips, one for each side of the chevron design. Side strips can be anywhere from 1″ (2.5cm) to 2-$\frac{1}{2}''$ (6.3cm) wide. Vary the widths of the side strips as you build the jacket. Pin strips right sides together to either side of the center chevron band, reversing the nap of the strips so the nap will be different from the outsides of the diagonal band. Sew using a $\frac{1}{4}''$ (6mm) seam. Sew both sides from the top down to keep from distorting the bands.

SEMINOLE INDIAN PATCHWORK COAT

Press bands open and pin to the backing. This is your basic sew-and-flip maneuver. See Fig. 3-19 showing the sew and flip on a different design. Using another side strip of a different dimension, reverse the nap and sew as before to the last sewn strip. Press and pin. You now have the center band sewn with two side strips on each side of the band. For samples of patchwork strips ready to be sewn, see Fig. 3-20.

Lay out remaining Seminole bands to see where you will use each. I had enough nine patch to use two rows on the back and a row on each sleeve. I used Design #1 on both fronts. It does not make any difference how you use the Seminole. At this stage you are checking to be sure you have enough Seminole design yardage with which to work.

Let's return to the back of the jacket. Add the second Seminole band you have chosen and remember to sew from the same direction no matter how much easier it may seem to sew one side from the bottom. Roll up the right side of the jacket as you sew the left side. Be sure the Seminole band is flat and pinned to the backing cor-

rectly. Continue in this manner to fill the width of your back.

A speedier way to work is to pin strips on each of the five pattern backings at one time. Sit and sew each strip, get up, press, pin, and then plan the next sequence on all pieces, until all of the five pieces are filled with corduroy.

■ Fitting

Trim the five pieces. Check fitting and make adjustments as you did in the jacket made with one fabric in Chapter 2.

■ Machine Quilting

Cut lining, using the completed and fitted pieces of your outer shell as a pattern. Add $\frac{1}{2}''$ (1.3cm) extra to the sides and top and an extra 2″ (5cm) at the bottom of the sleeves, front, and back. Cut batting to match lining. Make your five sandwiches.

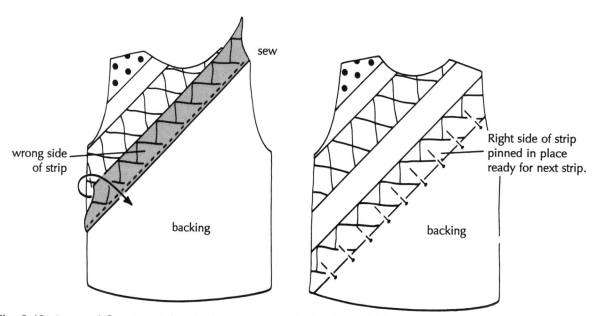

Fig. 3-19. *Sew and flip. A straight edge is necessary on both pieces of fabric—the piece you are adding and the piece to which you are adding. The added piece can be a rectangle, wedge shape, or a combination of fabrics sewn together with a final straight edge.*

Fig. 3-20. *Barbara Wollan's samples of 100-percent Seminole Indian patchwork made in my workshop. From top: two-strata design, design segments set between strips, square set on point, Design #1 with wide strips added.*

Quilting the Seminole makes the pattern look more complex than it is and this is where the fun begins. Your pattern "tells" you the design to use. Notice in the quilting diagram (Fig. 3-21) that in places I used the machine under control (feed dogs up) with the even-feed foot on the machine and in other places I used the machine free (feed dogs down). You can quilt this whole design with the feed dogs up if you wish. I use a 100/16 needle or a jeans needle in the machine and thread in a matching color. I like to use similar colors of thread and fabric in the lining as the outer shell so when quilting there is no chance of tension problems and some color showing on the wrong

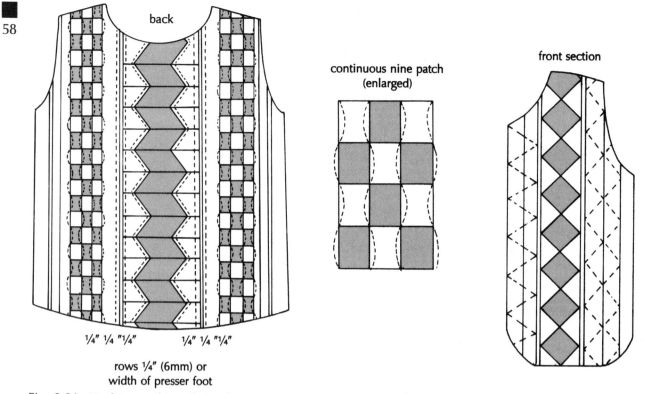

back

continuous nine patch
(enlarged)

front section

¼" ¼ "¼"   ¼" ¼ "¼"

rows ¼" (6mm) or
width of presser foot

Fig. 3-21. *Machine quilting design for a Seminole coat. The machine quilting on the coat was sewn with the even-feed foot and the feed dogs up. Each row started at the top and ended at the bottom of the coat. Pieces were marked with a template, or you can mark dots at equal distances down the line and eyeball from dot to dot. Nine-patch piece is done in Barbara-Johannah-style machine quilting with feed dogs down. You can stitch more rows starting in dark areas.*

places. If there is a big difference in color between the outer shell and lining I use invisible thread.

Note: I do find the even-feed foot bulky and sometimes makes it difficult to see where to stitch accurately. Recently two students in a class said they leave their even-feed foot on the machine all the time. They also automatically increase the stitch length when they turn their machines on for easier ripping.

A little housekeeping: My many bobbins are stored on large yellow-headed pins on a styrofoam Christmas tree, and I have tags with strings (similar to dress tags) that have needle numbers on them. When I change needles, I place a corresponding tag on the thread spool. I do the same with serger needles. The tags are stored in the same box as the needles.

■ Construction

This coat is finished exactly like the jacket made with plain fabric in Chapter 2.

Note: It's fun to vary this coat/jacket and use some strips of cotton velveteen with the corduroy. The pattern I used for my coat was an old Butterick 4506 pattern with the lapped front. I only used batting in the shoulder and 18" (45.7cm) down the backs and fronts. Any of the instructions in the book can be converted to other coverups.

CHAPTER 4

■ ■ ■

Other Pieced Jackets

In making the corduroy Seminole jacket, you have now experienced one piecing procedure. Other piecing methods are not much different. See the color section. Get out your scraps and let's consider what you need to think through.

Assemble similar scraps that you want to use together. Throw fabrics in piles on the floor. Stand back and look. Maybe wait a day or two. Ask yourself the following questions: Are these colors I will wear? Can all the fabrics used in the project be laundered the same way? Is everything preshrunk? Are colors all of the same tone, either all cool colors or all warm, or a pleasing mixture? Do I have a special section of pieced design that I want to feature? Have I considered the possibilities of all types of fabrics (silk neckties, velveteen, corduroy, leather, suede, woolens, silks, lamé, brocade, etc.)? Are the fabrics I want to use within my sewing ability? For example, forget knits for piecing projects. They can be used together to make leisure wear, but require different sewing techniques. What new piecing method do I want to try: cording, tucks, prairie points, Seminole Indian patchwork, a certain quilt block, or curved strip piecing? Do I have some special trims, ribbons, buttons, or laces that I want to incorporate?

The planning stage is a wonderful place for your imagination to blossom. Decision making is not easy, but each time you plan and execute a new garment, the process gets easier and the satisfaction greater. All it takes is a fresh initiative. This is a good place to review the "Design Principles" in Chapter 7.

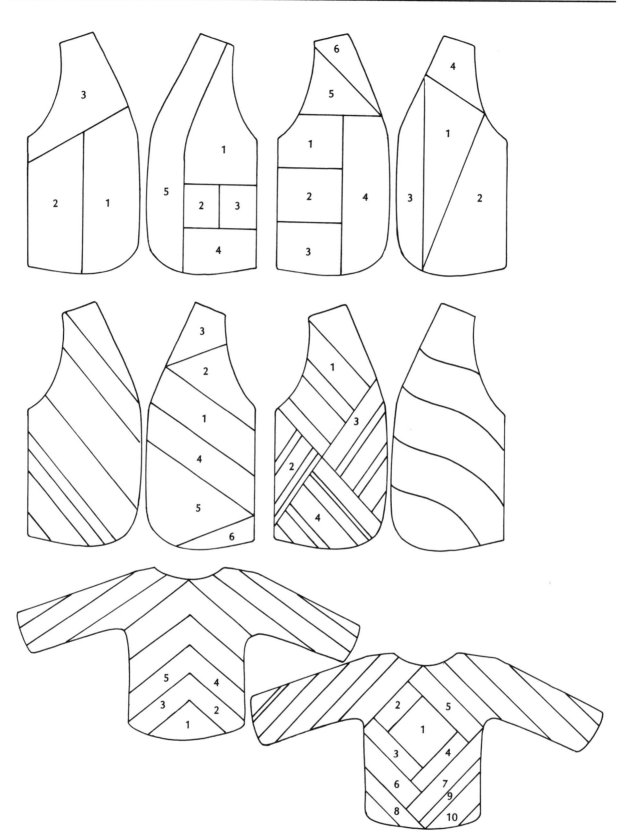

Fig. 4-1. *Ideas for pieced design placement. The numbers indicate the sewing sequence. Having a plan will save you the difficulty of working an area in with top stitching.*

MAKING PIECED JACKETS AND COATS

■ Placement of Design

Cut out your five backing pieces for a jacket or three pieces for a vest. Consider the possible piecing arrangements shown on Fig. 4-1. The numbers on the drawings indicate which section is finished first so that edges of that area can be covered with a straight piece. You can get in a bind and have to finish an area by folding a strip and finishing with top stitching. It's much better to plan the next section with a straight edge, no inside curves. Let's use an example to show what I mean. See Fig. 4-2 and Fig. 4-3. On the jacket in Fig. 4-2, I placed the enlarged Seminole blocks first and pieced around them. That left me to finish the v section to tie the whole thing together. The area is finished with a combination of hand and machine stitching. I was not happy about the ar-

Fig. 4-2. Jacket with enlarged Seminole block and continuous prairie points; design band is a variation of Seminole Design #1. Made of 100-percent cotton and quilted directly to the lining. Invisible thread on top; off-white thread in bobbin. Feed dogs up for quilting in ditch and straight areas and down for flower motifs in plain areas. Flower motif drawn from a template of light-weight cardboard that copies the flower in the print. 1990.

OTHER PIECED JACKETS

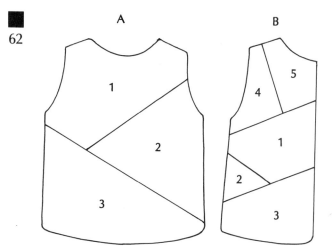

A   B

Fig. 4-3. *A difficult sewing sequence. Sew in order or you may have trouble. There are many different sequences to sew the sections of these two designs.*

rangement. In Fig. 4-3, if you sew area 3, then area 1, there is no way to sew area 2 easily. Plan ahead. Gather and record other placement ideas from books and periodicals (listed in the Bibliography).

Hint: Sometimes you want a design to flow from front to back. See the photograph of the tunic in the color section. In making the tunic I sewed the backing fronts to the back before adding the piecing, leaving the shoulders open. That gave me a larger flat piece to build on.

■ Construction

Draw lines on your backing pieces to show your design sections and indicate by numbers which areas to stitch first. Most stitching is a simple sew and flip maneuver. Place right sides together, sew, flip, press, and pin—ready for the next piece. Sometimes you will sew two or three pieces together separately and apply them to the batting. For example, you might sew a Seminole band with side strips. Do not sew too much away from the backing or it will be difficult to place the section on the backing properly and get it pressed smoothly. For a first project, do not make your pieces too small. Later you will find using many

pieces cause the colors to blend together and form a harmony with its own character.

It saves time and helps with color distribution to work on all five pieces of the garment at one time. Add new pieces to all five garment pieces. Sew five pieces, press five pieces, and continue. It's easier still to have a friend sewing while you arrange and press.

When your pieces are finished, the jacket is finished just like the plain jacket in Chapter 2 (pages 26–35). A vest can be easily lined following the vest lining directions in Chapter 7 (page 134).

■ Machine Quilting

More comments on machine quilting your pieces are in order. You have been given one example in the corduroy jacket and some general rules in the plain jacket example. With complicated lines of piecing, straight quilting through the jacket may not be attractive. I am usually not very happy with my piecing efforts until I quilt the pieces. The quilting gives the pieces depth, creating another layer of design. It is my favorite part of the process. The tactile feel of the sandwich has something to do with my satisfaction with the garment. I may be crazy but my better pieces seem to gain a personality and spirit all their own by the time they are completed. My creative energies are transferred to the item as I work on it.

■ Quilting Rules

1. A stitch length of 8-to-10 (2–3mm) stitches per inch is good.

2. Use your decorative stitches to quilt. This is best with smaller pieces since the decorative stitches take longer to form. However, you may have more patience than I.

3. Stitching in the ditch is one way to quilt without having to mark. See Fig. 4-4, part 3. Stitch around the seams of pieced areas. This works well with Seminole patchwork, which is too heavy to quilt through the designs.

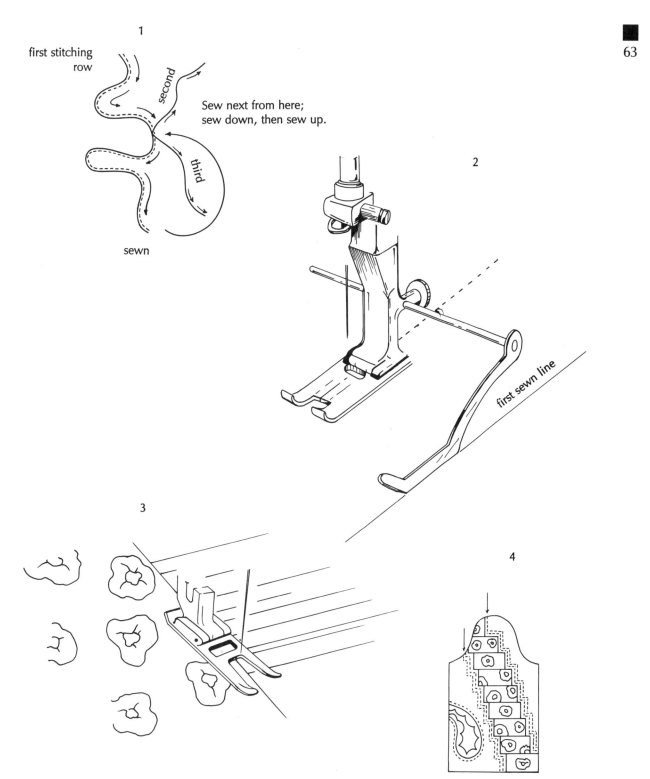

Fig. 4-4. *More quilting rules. 1. When sewing from a previously stitched line, set your stitch length at zero before beginning the second row. 2. Use a quilting guide in position to sew equally spaced rows. 3. Stitch in the ditch between two stitched rows. Pull the fabric apart and you can sew on the stitched row. 4. An example of how I stitched the sleeve on a pieced jacket by letting the design "talk" to me (shown is sleeve of jacket #7 in the color section).*

OTHER PIECED JACKETS

4. Use twin needles to make interesting patterns with simple designs. See your machine instruction book for turning with twin needles.

5. Use the same color thread in the bobbin and top when practical. This prevents the color of the bobbin thread from appearing on the top or the top thread color from traveling to the lining if the machine tension is not balanced exactly. Use color in the bobbin and invisible thread on top, or use invisible thread on top *and* in the bobbin. There are so many choices.

6. Vary the color of the thread for interest, and vary the weight of the thread by the following method. On a large, plain area to be quilted, baste the outline. Draw your design on the back within the basted area. Fill the bobbin with embroidery floss or perle cotton. Stitch from the back. Bring the thread ends to the back and tie. Some machines have a tension bypass for the bobbin and some machines work better with a separate bobbin case for heavier threads. *Do not* change the tension on the bobbin. If you ever have to hunt for that tiny screw on the floor, you will know why.

7. Use decorative threads on the top; metallics and rayons work well for a dressier look.

8. To anchor thread ends do one of three things: Bring thread ends to the back and tie, or stitch in place (with machine stitch length set at 0), or start by stitching tiny stitches and then lengthen. Put a dab of stitch sealant on the knot. Do not backstitch. One of the first things I machine-quilted was log cabin place mats and I backstitched them. The stitching wore first at the backstitched areas.

9. If your thread jams on the back when you are starting in the middle, take one stitch, pull the bobbin thread to the top, and hold it as you start. Some machines do not start smoothly if you are not holding the threads out to the side.

10. When using polyester batting (review types of batting in Chapter 2's Shopping List), quilting needs only to be 3″ (7.5cm) apart, or the width of your hand made into a fist. With cotton batting your quilting must be closer to prevent the batting from shifting when laundered.

11. Have an assortment of cardboard and plastic templates (circles, curves, triangles, etc.) on hand to help you get started. Collect lightweight cardboard ready to make more templates.

12. If you start quilting in the center of a garment, go back to that line to start the next line. Start from a previously quilted line. See Fig. 4-4, part 1.

13. Do not cross a quilted line more than once in the same place or you will get a bowed area.

14. Try to balance the amount of quilting over the whole piece.

15. Study Barbara Johannah's *Continuous Curve Quilting* (listed in the Bibliography) for ways to work around and through quilt blocks with the sewing machine.

16. Use the quilting guide that comes with most machines to measure parallel lines. See Fig. 4-4, part 2. Draw and stitch a line in the middle of your piece as a starting point. Measure and stitch the remaining lines with the quilting guide. The quilting guide can be moved to the left of the needle as well as positioned on the right.

Hint: The quilting guide won't fit on the even-feed foot or the darning foot. I use a small piece of cardboard and make my own guide. To do so, cut a piece of lightweight cardboard ¼″ (6mm) wide and the length of the width of the quilting rows you want *plus* ½″ (1.3cm). Fold one end up ¼″ (6mm) and attach it with duct tape to the right side of your even-feed foot about half-way back and ¼″ (6mm) from the bottom. Fold the second end of the strip down ¼″ (6mm). Practice stitching and adjust if necessary. You don't want the guide to touch the fabric; you want it to ride just above the fabric so you can stitch following your previously sewn line.

17. Your piecing design often will give you an idea of a quilting pattern. See Fig. 4-4, part 4 and the color section. The sleeve of this jacket has stair-step blocks and uses the width of the presser foot to quilt the second line. The zigzag pattern

was repeated for the rest of the sleeve. In the paisley print area, I quilted around the design with the feed dogs down.

18. Never pull hard on the fabric being quilted. Use gentle pressure with your hands flat on the bed of the machine.

19. Frequently check the back of your work for puckers. If you must rip, do so from the inside of your layers where there is less chance of harming your good fabrics.

20. Use your presser foot to measure lines when possible or use masking tape to mark lines. You may want to use $\frac{1}{4}''$ (6mm) masking tape to mark $\frac{1}{4}''$ (6mm) from the edge of your blocks.

The important thing is to get the work finished and have the satisfaction of doing it, and then be on your way to planning another project. I know designers who work out all their designs on paper first and follow them. I can not seem to visualize too far ahead. The process to me is as important as the product. I begin with the colors, a general idea, a stitching plan, and go from there. Some of my pieces do not work, but I learn from each mistake I make.

■ Finishing

All pieced jackets are finished (constructed) like the plain jacket in Chapter 2.

CHAPTER 5

■ ■ ■

Favorite Piecing and Embellishment Techniques

This section contains some of my favorite ways to add texture and interest to pieced clothing. If any of the ideas are new to you, I suggest you make a sample in your favorite colors. These pieces later can be incorporated into your piecing. Keep searching for new ideas for yourself. The designers who created these ideas found their inspiration in older clothing or ethnic clothing, or had enough experience in a technique to create new and faster construction methods. I look forward to the years to come so that I can practice more and keep finding new ideas.

■ Curved Strip Piecing

In *Curved Strip-Piecing: A New Technique* (see Bibliography for ordering), Marilyn Stothers has come up with a wonderful new way of piecing curves to make yardage for use in quilting projects. See the color section for a photograph of the tunic using curved strip piecing. The strip-pieced yardage you make can be used as it is or can be cut into shapes for your strip-pieced projects. (See next section on strip and string piecing.) Fig. 5-1 shows you a finished band with a template ready to cut a shape. Fig. 5-1 also shows you the completed block "Fascination" used in the tunic.

I have always preferred curves to straight lines and have tried sewing curves by marking, clipping, and using the flexible curve to cut curves. I've never been happy with any of these methods, until I tried Marilyn's new technique.

Choose four colors of 100-percent cotton for your pieced band. Use $\frac{1}{4}$ yd. (2.5dm) of each for experimenting. Prewash your fabric, straighten, fold once with selvages together and press. Stack your four colors on top of each other with folds

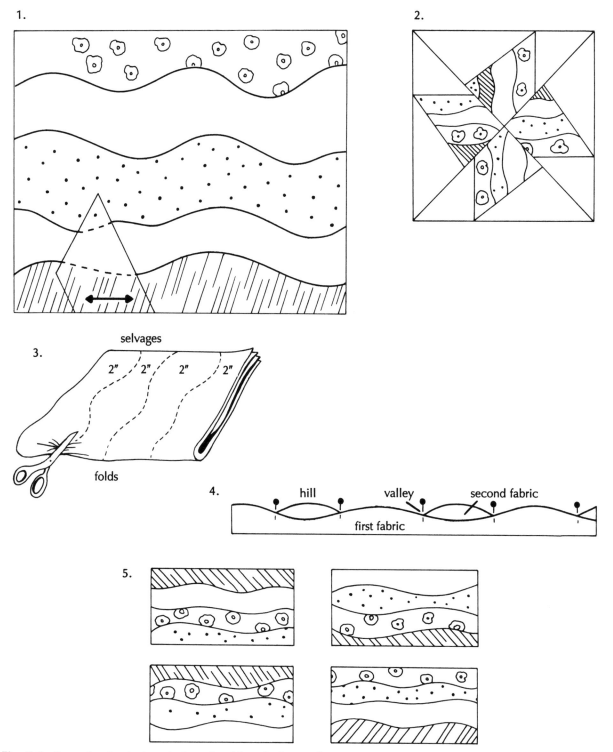

Fig. 5-1. *Curved strip piecing. 1. Completed band of curved strip piecing with template in position ready to mark and cut a shape. 2. The template shown is one used for the quilt block "Fascination." 3. Marking and cutting fabric for curved strip piecework. 4. Pinning two rows of cut curves together (used by permission of Marilyn Stothers). 5. Four finished bands of curved strip piecing.*

MAKING PIECED JACKETS AND COATS

together. Selvages won't necessarily meet because of the differences in fabric widths. Mark guidelines on the top piece of the fabric at selvages and fold the lines 2″ (5cm) apart using the disappearing pen. See Fig. 5-1 for layout and marking. With ¼ yd. (25cm) of fabric you will have four marks.

The next step is the designing done with your sharp scissors. Your aim is to cut *gentle* curves across the fabric from folds to selvages. (See Fig. 5-1.) Dotted lines on the drawing indicate possible cutting lines. Cut a long curve at the fold. Do not begin or end a curve at the fold. This is important. Keep your cut strips piled as you cut them and in the order of cutting.

On a large work area take the top cut strip, open it up, and lay it out. Take the second cut strip from the second cut pile. Take the third cut strip from the third pile and the bottom strip from the fourth pile. You should have a band laid out of four colors that will fit together. Start the second band with the top (second) color, and continue in this manner to lay out four bands.

You now are ready to pin and sew your bands. See drawing of pinning (Fig. 5-1). Place the first two strips right sides together. Start matching and pinning at the center hill and valley, matching the center fold lines on both strips exactly. The pins go at each valley, and the mountains are even across your row.

Take the first pinned set to the sewing machine, which is set up with thread that is similar to your colors. Use ¼″ (6mm) seams. Is your machine bed still marked for ¼″ (6mm) seams? I prefer to start sewing at the fold in the center. (Marilyn starts sewing at one end.) Put the needle down at ¼″ (6mm) to hold your work until you get your hands in position. Take out the next pin. Put the seams together. As you sew, you are gently using your fingers to ease the hills and valleys together. My fingers on my right hand go between the fabric in front of the needle. My left hand gently pulls. When wrinkles are about to go under the needle, raise the presser foot and straighten. It's important not to pull hard on these edges since they are all bias. You may find another way that's easier for you to position your hands. When you have sewn from the fold to one end, flip your

work and start sewing at the fold to the second end. Continue sewing until you have four bands. See Fig. 5-1 for finished bands.

Press seams in one direction from the back. Flip over and check that all seams are pulled to their full width. Spray starch is helpful here. Even if there is a little bowing in your first piece, you can cut out parts of it with a template.

You have created enough curved patchwork to begin a project. At least you will be able to see if you enjoy the method as I do. I started with nine colors and have enough piecework left for a second project.

Marilyn's book *Curved Strip-Piecing: A New Technique* includes complete directions for random, regular, and exact-measured pieces. You get all the information you need to continue creating curved strip piecework plus fine examples of curves used in piecing in her book.

■ Strip and String Piecing

Strip quilting is similar to Seminole Indian patchwork. Sew strata of varying random widths of fabric or preplanned strips. It's best to keep strip widths between ¾″ (2cm) and 2-½″ (7.5cm). I take straight pieces left from projects to make strata for future projects and usually have a bag of saved strips and sewn strata. Remember to reverse the direction of the strips when sewing your strata. You can make a strata as wide as you want. Fig. 5-2, Fig. 5-3, and Fig. 5-4 give you some ideas of how to use the strata. Figure 5-2 is called Bargello, Fig. 5-3 is Spiderweb, and Fig. 5-4 shows different ways to cut and use strata. See *Quick-and-Easy Strip Quilting* (listed in the Bibliography) for more ideas.

The following illustrations are examples of strip piecing: Fig. 5-5 (velveteen cape with string piece lining); Fig. 7-6 (boots); Fig. 5-16, Fig. 5-17 (Marie Wood's two tops); and Fig. 7-15, Fig. 7-16 (doodle cloths). In the color section see the jacket with crazy quilting, the string piecing on the back of a jacket), and strip-pieced quilt.

String quilting is similar to strip quilting, but

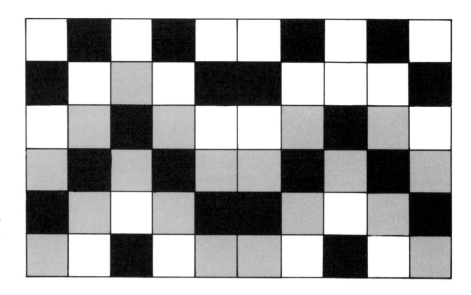

Fig. 5-2. *Bargello. Strata of varying length, width, and colors shifted up and down and resewn.*

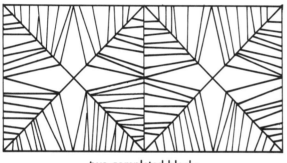

two completed blocks

¼ of block;
sides covered by strings

Fig. 5-3. *Spiderweb. An example of how strip and string piecing can be used in a quilt block. You can sew this block with three colors and no strip or string.*

you start with a fabric or paper base and add odd-sized pieces of leftover fabric in sew and flip. Here the strings can be straight or wedges as long as there is one straight edge onto which to add the next fabric. Crazy quilting is a form of string quilting. (See Dixie Haywood's *Crazy Quilting with a*

Difference, listed in the Bibliography). I like to take a piece of backing fabric about 3″ (7.5cm) wide and an undetermined length. Start in the middle and pin one piece of fabric right-side-up on the backing. On either side, pin another piece of fabric with right sides together. Each fabric has one straight side. Sew and flip. Continue working on both sides. Review Fig. 3-19 on how to sew and flip.

Any piece of a quilt block can be filled with strings and joined with the other block pieces. Silk neckties make great strings. Finished string pieces can be used in all the same ways as strip piecing noted previously.

Wonderful string piecing is shown in the fall 1990 *American Quilter* by Caryl Bryer Fallert. Caryl's work is very artistic and her directions are clear and easy to follow (see the color section).

Both strip and string methods are great for sewing unusual clothing and at the same time they use up scraps of fabric.

■ Afghani Piecework

Afghani piecework, a version of strip quilting, can decorate clothing or be incorporated into quilts or household items. You can plan the color of the piecework or randomly use your scraps of cotton and cotton/polyesters of comparable weight. My thanks to Yvonne Porcello, Margaret Dittman and

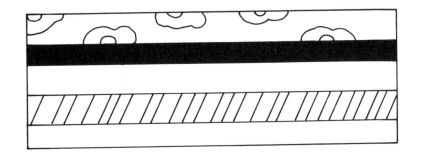

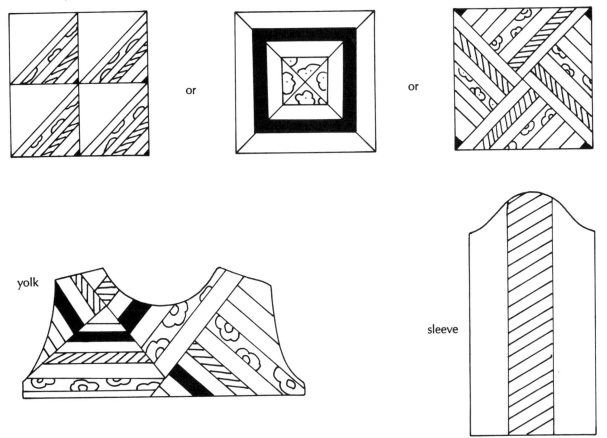

Roman stripe

yolk

sleeve

Fig. 5-4. *Cutting and using stripped fabric. A few examples to get you started thinking of the many possibilities. Top left piece is strata ready to be cut with a triangle template. Sew stripped triangle to plain triangle to create a Roman stripe. For bottom left example, trace pattern piece on paper, cut apart, add seam allowance to pieces, cut from strata, and resew.*

FAVORITE PIECING AND EMBELLISHMENT TECHNIQUES

Fig. 5-5. *Velveteen cape with strip-piece lining. Cape quilted directly to the batting and backing with matching thread. Quilting design from star-type quilt blocks. Lining not quilted. Lining and front attached by bias edging. Lining blocks made from scraps. 1987.*

their predecessors for information on this technique.

See Fig. 5-6 and the photograph of Afghani piecework on a jacket (Fig. 5-7).

Directions

Draft a unilateral triangle (equal length on three sides). You can use three rulers to do this. Try 2″ (5cm) sides or size of your choice. Cut a number of triangles of this size. Try this quick cutting method with your rotary cutter, mat, and Plexiglas ruler. Cut several strips of 1¾″ (4.4cm)

wide fabric. Stack them on top of each other. Draw your triangle on top layer. Cut all at once with the rotary cutter. See Fig. 5-6, part 2. This method works with many of your quilt pieces when you need multiples. For more information on this speedy cutting method, see an article by Helen Whitson Rose in the May 1990 *Quilter's Newsletter Magazine,* or her book *Quick-and-Easy Strip Quilting* (listed in the Bibliography).

Cut strips of another fabric or variety of fabrics. If your triangles are 2″ (5cm), your strips are cut 1″ (2.5cm) wide and 3″ (7.5cm) long. The proportion for the width of the strip is one-half

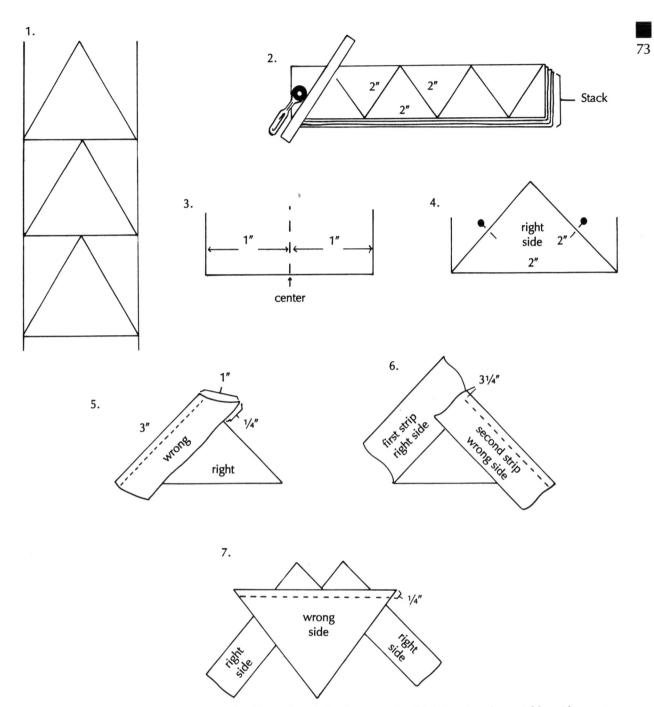

Fig. 5-6. *Afghani piecework. 1. Finished Afghani band. 2. Cut a stack of fabric triangles quickly with a rotary cutter. 3. Dimensions of base fabric. 4. Pin triangle. 5. Add first strip. 6. Add second strip. 7. Add second triangle.*

FAVORITE PIECING AND EMBELLISHMENT TECHNIQUES

Fig. 5-7. *Jacket with Afghani piecework and print fabric. Straight lines around piecework were quilted with the feed dogs up. Quilting in the print area uses invisible thread and feed dogs down. Separate lining is used because free stitching on the back is messy. Outer shell is made of 100-percent cotton; lining is polyester. 1989.*

the measurement of your triangle and for the length of the strip is the measurement of the triangle side plus 1″ (2.5cm).

An example of another size is a 3″ (7.5cm) unilateral triangle, strips 1-½″ (3.7cm) in width and 4″ (1dm) in length.

Draw the width of the triangle on a base strip of fabric. Draw a center line. The length of the base strip is the amount of piecework you want. See Fig. 5-6, part 3.

Hint: Instead of using a base strip, you can draw your lines directly onto the backing cut for a pieced jacket. Just plan where you want the piecework and draw parallel lines as wide as your triangles. Then sew directly onto the backing. The edges can be finished later by adding straight side strips.

Pin the first triangle on the base, right-side-up. See Fig. 5-6, part 4. Pin first strip to left edge of the triangle, right sides together, with end of strip ¼″ (6mm) above the point of the triangle. See Fig. 5-6, part 5. Sew and flip, then finger-press. Sew the second strip to the other side of the triangle, right sides together, ending ¼″ (6mm) above the point of the triangle. See Fig. 5-6, part 6. Sew and finger-press.

The second triangle is placed right-side-down so the top seam will meet the point of the first triangle. It helps to finger-press the seam allowance to use as a seam guide and to position it on the first triangle point. Sew & flip. See Fig. 5-6, part 7. Continue until the base is filled.

Hints:

1. If sewing on the machine, it is not necessary to cut the bobbin thread and seldom necessary to cut the upper thread. Just lift the presser foot with the needle in the upper position and pull your work to next sewing position. This is much faster.

2. Draw some parallel lines perpendicular to the outside edges of your base strip to give you a visual guide in keeping the triangles bases parallel.

3. Yvonne Porcello says she developed the method from examples of textiles from Afghan, Turkish, and Uzbe nomads. She taught the method to Margaret Dittman (*The Fabric Lover's Scrapbook,* listed in the Bibliography). Both women prefer to make the patchwork by hand.

■ Meadow Points

Meadow points are small, folded sections of fabric that look similar to prairie points except they are cut from a continuous fabric band and used in patterned rows. See the photograph on meadow points on the jacket back in the color section. See Fig. 5-8.

You may enjoy making this colorful band called meadow points to use in your jackets, vests, skirt bands, or on household items. The directions may look complicated but, working with the

fabric step by step, will give you results quickly. The following instructions will make a band 11″ (2.7dm) wide and 45″ (1.2m) long. Vary the dimensions to fit the length of your project. Use 100-percent cotton that does not fray easily. Preshrink all fabrics.

Cut five background color strips: three strips 1-¼″ (3.3cm) × 45″ (1.2m) and two strips 4″ (1dm) × 45″ (1.2m), the latter for the top and bottom strips. Use your rotary cutter for accuracy. The background strips are usually all the same color. Cut four colored strips: 2-½″ (6.2cm) × 45″ (1.2m). These colors will form the meadow points. Press each colored band in half lengthwise, right-sides-out. Spray starch on the bands helps in forming the points later.

Cutting and Sewing Order

Top strip:	4″ (1dm) × 45″ (1.2m) background color
Color strip:	2-½″ (6.2cm) × 45″ (1.2m) —fold in half
Background strip:	1-¼″ (3.1cm) × 45″ (1.2m) background color
Color strip:	2-½″ (6.2cm) × 45″ (1.2m) —fold in half
Background strip:	1-¼″ (3.1cm) × 45″ (1.2m) background color
Color strip:	2-½″ (6.2cm) × 45″ (1.2m) —fold in half
Background strip:	1-¼″ (3.1cm) × 45″ (1.2m) background color
Color strip:	2-½″ (6.2cm) × 45″ (1.2m) —fold in half
Bottom strip:	4″ (1dm) × 45″ (1.2m) background color

To sew strips together stack them as follows (see Fig 5-8, part 1): Place 4″ (1dm) background strip (top) on the work surface right-side-up. Stack one of the folded color strips on top, matching bottom raw edges. On top of the folded color strip, place one narrow (1-¼″ [3.3cm]) background strip. Sew through all three strips with a ¼″ (6mm) seam. See Fig. 5-8, part 2. This is a good place to

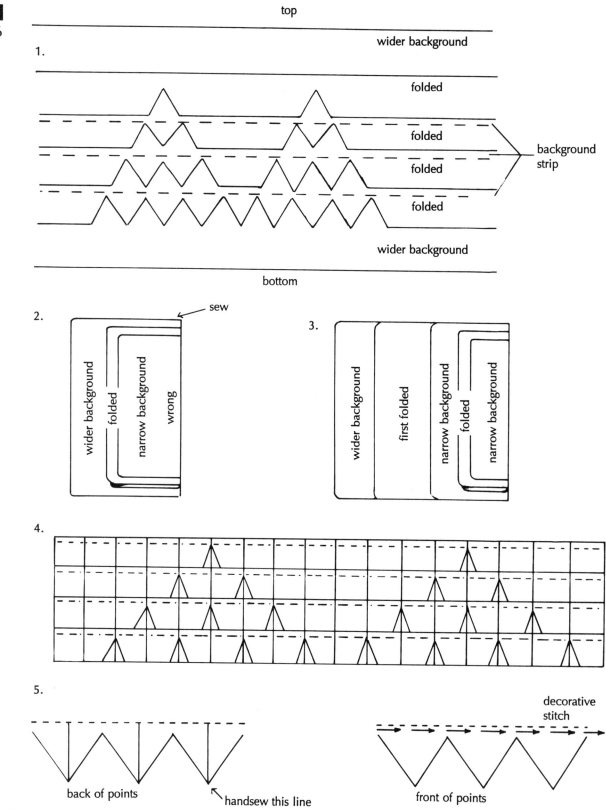

Fig. 5-8. *Meadow points. 1. View of finished band with folds marked. 2. Sew strips together. 3. View of second seam with directions. 4. Mark and clip completed band and clip at the v's. 5. Finished meadow points.*

MAKING PIECED JACKETS AND COATS

use your serger to make the back of your band neater. Just be sure to find an exact $\frac{1}{4}''$ (6mm) seam on your serger and to use four threads for sewing wovens. Open up the narrow background strip and place the second folded color strip on its bottom raw edge. Then stack a narrow background strip, aligning bottom raw edges. See Fig. 5-8, part 3. Sew. Continue in this manner and end with the widest background strip (bottom). You are alternating background strips and colored folded bands. See Fig. 5-8, part 4 and the cutting and sewing chart.

Press the band from the back with the seams going upward. To mark and clip the meadow points, first measure the width of a finished folded band. Use this as the measurement for marking across the entire band vertically. Use a disappearing pencil to mark. In this example the marks will be 1″ (2.5cm) apart if your measurements were accurate. Mark each folded band at 1″ (2.5cm) intervals as shown. See Fig. 5-8, part 4. Clip vertically to the stitching in the folded bands. Clip only those marked lines indicated on the pattern to make the design.

Press up points as the drawing shows. You are folding the fabric up and under at a 45-degree angle on either side of the cut. See Fig. 5-8, part 5. The points either can be hand-stitched or pinned and stitched with a decorative machine stitch along the top of the points. Make sure to catch the top edge of the folded points. Even if you are hand stitching, you may want to stitch a row of decorative stitches to prevent fraying when you wash the article.

Variations

These are the dimensions I used on the back of the jacket in color section 6. For background strips: three strips at $4\frac{1}{2}''$ (1.1dm) × 45″ (1.2m), two strips at 6″ (1.5dm) × 45″ (1.2m) for the top and bottom. Colored strips: four at 5″ (1.2dm). This made a band 27″ (6.7dm) wide. Create your own variations.

Another variation is to use one color throughout for a subtle textural effect. I saw a christening dress in Virginia with tiny white meadow points that was simply beautiful.

For help and inspiration in making meadow points I owe special thanks to Margaret Dittman's *The Fabric Lover's Scrapbook* (Chilton Book Company, 1988) and *Tomorrow's Heirlooms,* Joan Padgett, (1301 W. Hwy. 407, Suite 202, Lewisville, TX 75067, 1986-Kit).

■ Continuous Prairie Points

Prairie points are squares of fabric folded to make a fabric triangle. It is an interesting way to finish the edges of quilts and to add textural interest in piecing garments.

Fig. 5-9 shows continuous prairie points with the following directions: 1) continuous (above) and traditional (below) points; 2) marking and cutting for continuous prairie points; 3) folding and pinning; 4) construction of continuous prairie points. The box shows traditional prairie points construction methods #1 and #2. Illustrations are taken from *Quilter's Newsletter Magazine* (no. 215), which shows techniques developed by Eleanor Burenheide. See the jacket in Fig. 4-2 with prairie points incorporated in the design.

Let's make a sample to see how easy the method is. Cut a 10″ (2.5dm) wide band of 100-percent cotton with a length of 22″ (5.5dm). Fold and press the band in half lengthwise, wrong sides together.

Open the band on your work space with the wrong side up. Mark off 5″ (1.2dm) sections on the wrong side of the fabric, perpendicular to the right-hand long edge of the band and continuing to the fold. On the left hand side, mark 5″ (1.2 dm) sections across from the middle of a right-hand section, like shingles. You will have 5″ (1.2dm) sections on one side and 5″ (1.2dm) sections one half way in between first 5″ (1.2dm) sections. See Fig. 5-9, part 2. Cut drawn lines very carefully to the fold, but not through the fold.

Work on the ironing board to press as you go. Press points as in Fig. 5-9, part 3. Fold lower right corner A up to fold line at B. Then fold point C to point D, forming a triangle. Go to the other side, fold twice, and press. Fold the first triangle

1.

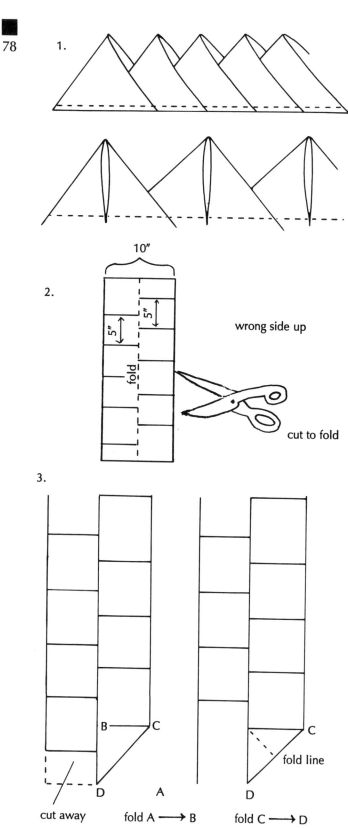

2.

10"

5"

5"

fold

wrong side up

cut to fold

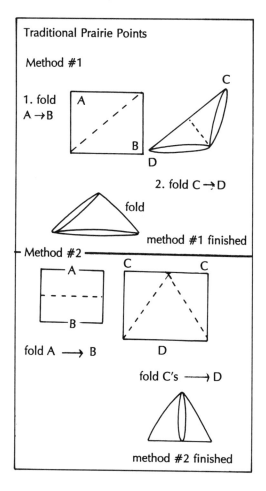

Traditional Prairie Points

Method #1

1. fold
A → B

2. fold C → D

fold

method #1 finished

Method #2

fold A → B

D

fold C's → D

method #2 finished

3.

B — C

D

A

cut away

fold A → B

fold line

C

D

fold C → D

4.

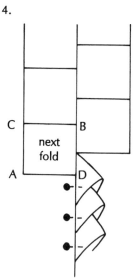

C

B

next
fold

A

D

Fig. 5-9. *Continuous and traditional prairie points.*

MAKING PIECED JACKETS AND COATS

into the second triangle. Continue folding triangles, alternating sides until the end of the band is reached. See Fig. 5-9, part 4. Pin each junction. Baste on the machine $\frac{1}{4}''$ (6mm) from the edge to hold folds in place until you are ready to use them. Insert the bands into a seam in your piecing.

You can vary the width of your strips and thus the size of the prairie points. Your drawing measurement is always one-half the size of the band. Thus on an 8" (2dm)-wide band, mark at 4" (1dm) intervals.

With continuous prairie points, it is not possible to vary the size of the points within the band as it would be making one prairie point at a time. See Fig. 5-9 inset box for the traditional way to make prairie points.

■ Quilt Blocks

There are many good books to help you make traditional quilt blocks by quicker, sewing-machine methods. (See the Bibliography.) I don't want to say much about them except to mention two methods and to stress the need for accuracy in piecing. See Fig. 5-10.

We already have talked about Seminole Indian patchwork (Chapter 3) and you have drawings of a square block made the Seminole way. (See Fig. 4-2, which shows a jacket containing an enlarged Seminole design.) My blocks or graph-paper blocks you draw yourself are wonderful resources for larger blocks.

Designing Your Own Enlarged Seminole Block

Decide on the block size you want and draw the block on graph paper with one block of graph paper equal to $\frac{1}{4}''$ (6mm). With colored pencils, color blocks to indicate different fabrics.

Draw dotted lines on your graph to represent the strata needed. Three strata in a block is enough to handle easily. Draw each strata to the side of the larger drawing. Add seam allowance.

You will begin to look at quilt blocks in a different way, and think of ways to use the Seminole (strip) method to make construction easier.

As an example, see Fig. 5-11, a Seminole block used in the skirt pictured in the color section. The block on the skirt is rectangular rather than square, and the drawing is correct. Why aren't the blocks square? I doubled all the dimensions from a smaller Seminole design, including the seam allowances. Mary Scroggs from Chapel Hill showed me my mistake. By doubling the smaller Seminole blocks, you end up with too much seam allowance. Draw your design square on graph paper and *then* add seam allowance.

The width of the rectangles used to form triangles to set the blocks on point is the width of your block plus $\frac{1}{2}''$ (1.3cm) seam allowance. If you wanted to set the example shown in Fig. 5-11 on point, this measurement would be 6-$\frac{1}{2}''$ (1.6dm). To get the length of the rectangle, measure the block diagonally (8-$\frac{1}{2}''$ [2.1dm]) and add 1" (2.5cm) for two $\frac{1}{2}''$ (1.3cm) seam allowances. Review Fig. 3-15 for setting on point and see that you cut into the rectangle between the blocks $\frac{1}{2}''$ (1.3cm) instead of $\frac{1}{4}''$ (6mm). The subtitle of this book should be "Learn with Nancy."

In *Wearable Art for Real People,* Mary Mashuta gives a much better way to make a quilt block for clothing. The method is better because the units are smaller, and the smaller the pieces in piecing, the better the garment looks. Draw a number of 3" (7.5cm) × 5" (1.2dm) blocks. Divide the blocks with three or more straight lines. See Fig. 5-12. Choose two or three blocks you like and make templates for the shapes within them, remembering to add seam allowances. Use these modules to create your jacket or vest. You can, of course, change the size of the module to have fewer pieces and instead of straight lines use curved lines. Mary has some interesting color theories and her work with stripes is wonderful, like a cheating strip piecing (taking preprinted striped material instead of saving your own strips).

I cut existing blocks made with marbleized fabric and crazy quilting into 3" (7.5cm) × 5" (1.2dm) blocks to use in piecing the jacket shown in the photograph in the color section. Thank you, Mary, for your inspiration.

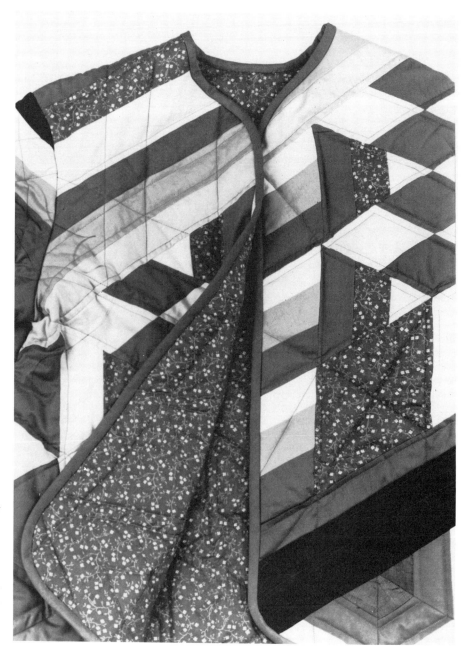

Fig. 5-10. *Jacket with parts of diamond quilt blocks, made of 100-percent cotton. Lining features a print fabric. The back was hand-quilted $\frac{1}{4}''$ (6mm) from the diamonds. Feed dogs were up for front-machine quilting. 1988.*

strata

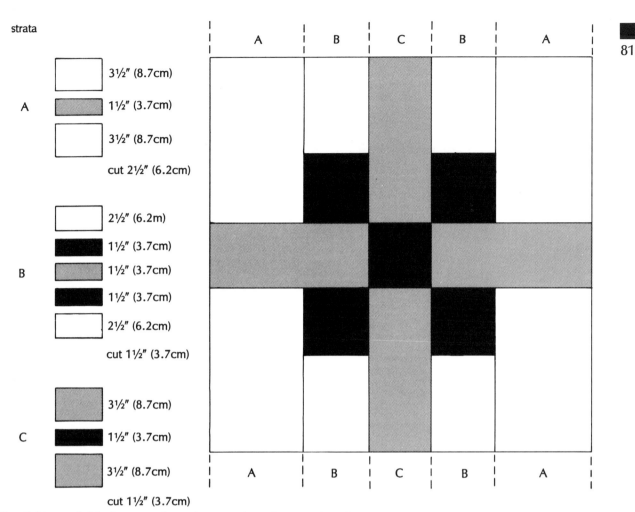

A
- 3½" (8.7cm)
- 1½" (3.7cm)
- 3½" (8.7cm)

cut 2½" (6.2cm)

B
- 2½" (6.2m)
- 1½" (3.7cm)
- 1½" (3.7cm)
- 1½" (3.7cm)
- 2½" (6.2cm)

cut 1½" (3.7cm)

C
- 3½" (8.7cm)
- 1½" (3.7cm)
- 3½" (8.7cm)

cut 1½" (3.7cm)

Fig. 5-11. *Quilt blocks. An enlarged Seminole Indian patchwork.*

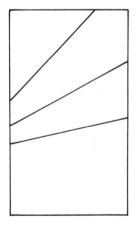

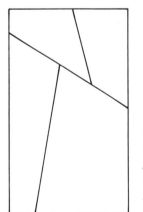

Fig. 5-12. *Smaller quilt modules (3" [7.5cm] × 5" [12.5cm]) made with three lines. Used by permission of Mary Mashuta from* Wearable Art for Real People.

FAVORITE PIECING AND EMBELLISHMENT TECHNIQUES

Koss Method of Appliqué

An article by David Page Coffin in *Threads* (December 1989/January 1990), introduced us to Koss van den Akker, an inventive clothing designer who uses a fun approach to appliquéd clothing. He cuts his pattern pieces in a designer fabric, then uses a wide array of print fabrics cut in shapes to apply to the garment. The raw edges of the shapes are covered by flattened bias tubes formed from another fabric. The look is a wonderful blend of color and texture. Celtic designs and stained glass work in patchwork are similar techniques.

Yards of bias are made for Koss by a company in New York. The bias is appliquéd on both edges to the shapes on the clothing, being careful to make inside and outside corners sharp turns. The jacket shown in the color section is my second attempt at this technique. The first jacket is not finished, but the third is planned, just waiting for

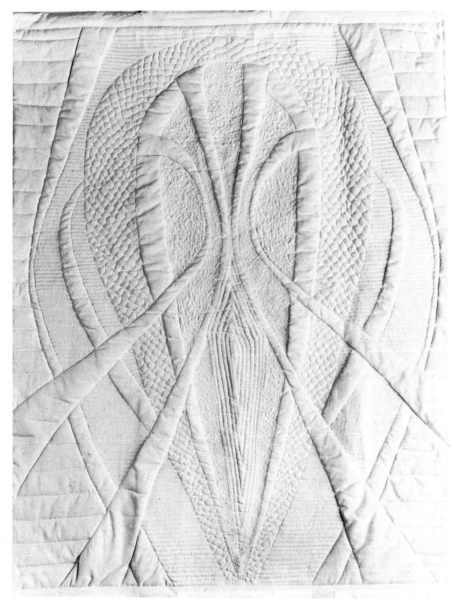

Fig. 5-13. *White hanging that serves as a sampler of dense stitching. The design was taken from a magazine picture of a lamp base. I intend to use this design for another Koss-style jacket. Made of 100-percent cotton. 1989.*

Autumn Aurora by Caryl Fallert. String pieced with hand-dyed silk. 1988.

Yvonne Porcello's work. My favorite piecer, "How Old Are You Now?" was made for the Fairfield/Concord fashion show, 1988/89, and features cotton fabrics.

String-quilted and black jacket made of 100-percent cotton. String patchwork was made directly between drawn parallel lines on the backing. Cording was added to sides of the string areas. The jacket was quilted with black thread, feed dogs up and even-feed foot. Templates used were an assortment of half-moon shapes made from lightweight cardboard. 1989.

Jacket made of 100-percent cotton with meadow points on top back. The 3" × 5" (7.5cm × 12.5cm) blocks were cut from larger blocks using self-dyed marbleized fabric. This fabric was made in a workshop taught by Anne Weaver and a crazy quilt workshop taught by Dixie Haywood. Quilted with invisible thread on top and lavender in bobbin, feed dogs up for straight quilting, mostly quilting in the ditch, and feed dogs down for quilting around paisley shapes in print fabric. 1990.

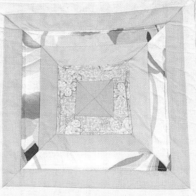

Guest room quilt made of cottons, 72" × 64". Strata was made on the serger, and the blocks were sewn together on a regular machine. Strip quilt design, 72" × 64" (18m × 1.5m). Quilting is explained in Chapter 5. 1988.

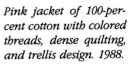

Pink jacket of 100-percent cotton with colored threads, dense quilting, and trellis design. 1988.

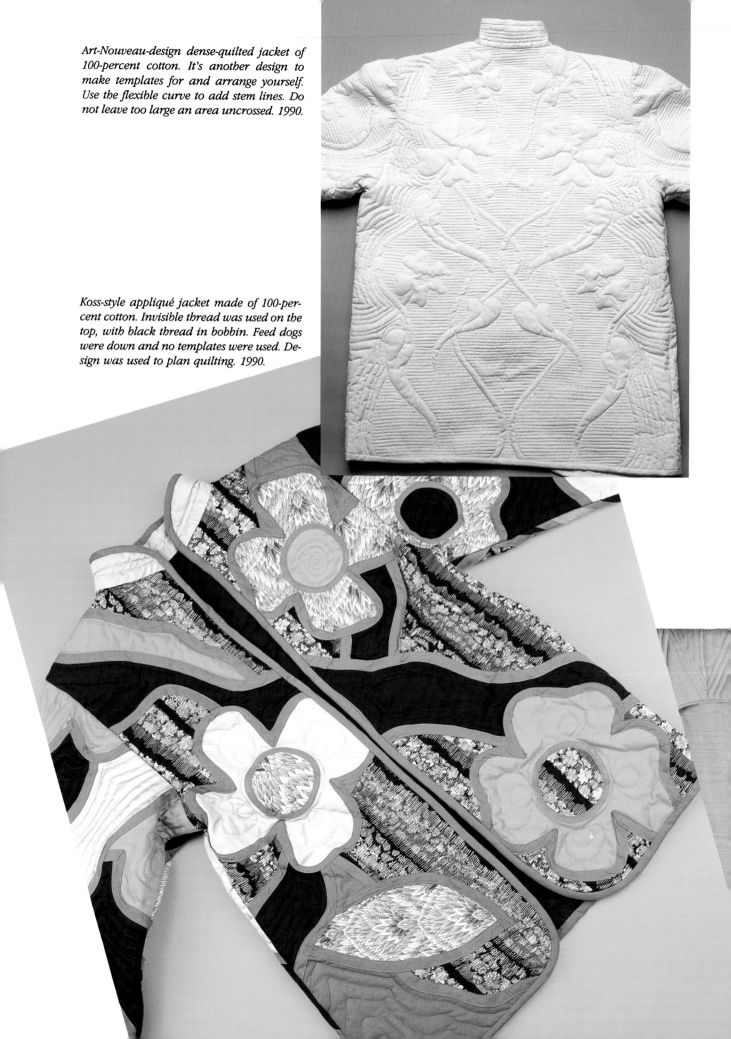

Art-Nouveau-design dense-quilted jacket of 100-percent cotton. It's another design to make templates for and arrange yourself. Use the flexible curve to add stem lines. Do not leave too large an area uncrossed. 1990.

Koss-style appliqué jacket made of 100-percent cotton. Invisible thread was used on the top, with black thread in bobbin. Feed dogs were down and no templates were used. Design was used to plan quilting. 1990.

Procion-dyed jacket of 100-percent cotton with flowers. It was quilted with feed dogs down and following the pattern of the fabric. 1985. Owner: Gretchen Young.

Paisley dense-design jacket of 100-percent cotton overdyed with procion dyes. I used muslin from two different bolts, and the shades were different. I tried tea dye and bleach to cover my goof and finally dyed the entire jacket. The paisley design is best done by making assorted-sized templates. This is a good sampler of different dense stitches. The crosshatch dense stitch was used for the background. 1985.

Detail of wool cape with wool outer shell and polyester lining. Design and construction are explained in the text. 1990.

Lavender corduroy jacket of one fabric featuring lavender cotton lining, lavender thread, and feed dogs up with even-feed foot. Design drawn with dressmaker's curve. 1990. Owner: Marilyn Held.

Skirt of 100-percent cotton made by my daughter, Elizabeth Chalk. Enlarged Seminole Indian patchwork border. Skirt construction is described in Chapter 3. 1990.

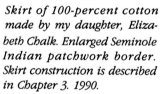

Seminole Indian patchwork coat made of corduroy with pewter buttons. Outer shell is cotton and polyester; the lining is cotton. Quilted with feed dogs both up and down. Complete directions are in Chapter 3. 1989.

Dusty rose jacket and skirt featuring all-over dense quilting design; cotton and polyester outer fabric, and polyester lining. The jacket is a Laura Ashley pattern. No batting in upper sleeve, but quilting line continues into upper sleeve. Horizontal dense stitch was sewn vertically. 1987.

Tunic made of 100-percent cotton, with curved strip piecing used in quilt block and sections by itself. Barbara Johannah-style quilting (see Bibliography) was used around quilt blocks with feed dogs up and even-feed foot on. Curved areas were quilted with feed dogs down, directly to the lining. Lightweight batting was used. 1990.

Silk jacket and jump suit made from a design created by my mother while she was a student at Carnegie Tech in the 1920s. She used the design of a silk top on the sleeve and worked it in crewel embroidery. This jacket was stitched with rayon thread. 1990.

time to sew it. The design I plan to use next time is the dense-quilted wall hanging in Fig. 5-13.

Koss's method is not as easy as it looks, and I learned several things in the process.

1. It is very important to cut true bias. The rotary cutter and board make the cutting easier.

2. Bias tape makers come in different sizes and are small pieces of metal that turn the seam allowances of the bias as you press. (See the Supply List for notions companies that sell them.) It takes practice to make the bias smoothly. You must put tension on the strip as you hold the bias maker and press. The tension is best held by anchoring the end of the strip with a pin. Use a pressing, not ironing, technique with your iron: Lift up and set down. My bias tape maker makes $\frac{1}{2}''$ (1.3cm) bias, but I plan to get the 1″ (2.5cm) bias tape maker to see if that can make it more neatly.

3. Make the design *simple*. My first attempt was a flower form with too many angles. The second, shown in the color section, was not much simpler and resulted in the bias not being as neat as I would like.

4. Be very sure that you catch the edge of your appliqué shape with the bias. It's best to sew the inside part of the bias next to the shape first. Form your curves with the iron before applying.

5. Try Unique Stitch or No More Pins adhesives to hold the bias in place before sewing.

6. Use Fasturn to turn a sewn bias seam. This is a handy product that easily turns fabric tubes right-side-out. Press seam to the middle of the underside. If you sew straight, you can ensure a bias strip of equal width. This method gives the neatest results. Fasturn (shown in Fig. 5-14) is a collection of tubes and wires that simplifies making tubes of various sizes. Good directions come with the product and new uses still are being discovered.

7. Try sewing a $\frac{1}{4}''$ (6mm) seam in the bias, wrong sides together, leaving the seam on the outside. Then press the seam to the middle of the underside. This way the bias also will be of equal width.

8. I have a set of plastic heat-proof strips called Unique Markers that can be inserted in a sewn bias seam, either inside or outside, to press the seam. Metal heat-proof guides called Celtic Bars are also on the market.

This information gives you many ways to experiment making bias tubes. You will learn there are many uses for them.

Naturally, when I finished piecing my Koss jacket, I wanted to quilt it. Koss does not quilt his, but give the method a try. If it doesn't work, you can cut up the fabric and use it as 3″ (7.5cm) × 5″ (1.2dm) blocks described in the last section. Nothing ever goes to waste.

See the interesting pieced garments made by Marie Wood. Do they give you any ideas? See Figs. 5-15 and 5-16.

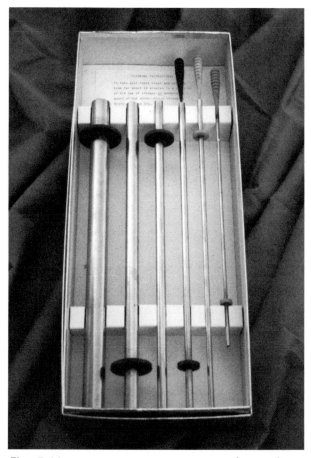

Fig. 5-14. *Fasturn. A great way to make cordings, braids, stuffed toys, belts, and jewelry. New uses are constantly being discovered. Fasturn consists of six tubes and three wires of different sizes. Good directions come with the set.*

Fig. 5-15. *Marie Wood of Salisbury made this strip-pieced pullover from a pattern by Lassie Whittman. To order the pattern, write to Lassie Whittman, P.O. Box 774, Rochester, WA 98579.*

MAKING PIECED JACKETS AND COATS

Fig. 5-16. *A second Marie Wood garment. The pattern was designed by Bonnie Benson. Marie added her own touches to the strip piecing. 1990. To order the pattern, write to Quilter's Resource, Inc., P.O. Box 148850, Chicago, IL 60614 or see the Porcella books listed in the Bibliography.*

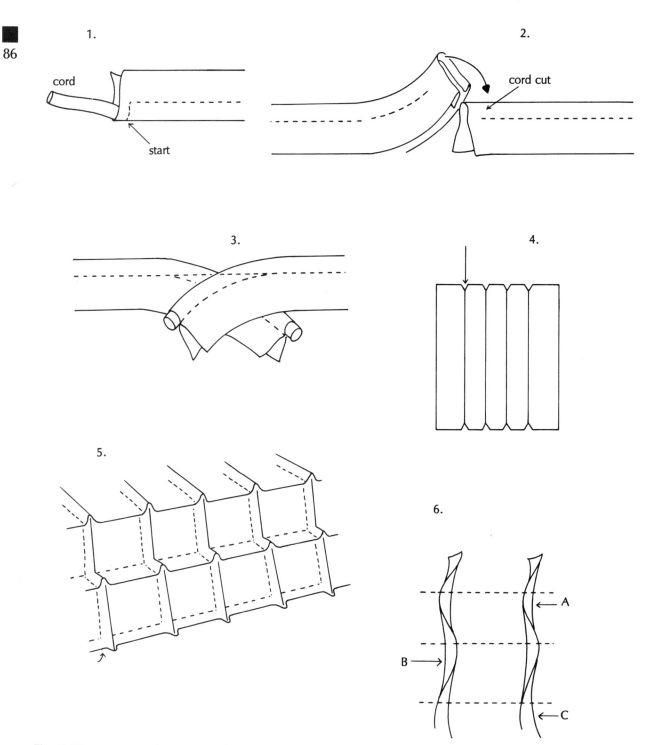

Fig. 5-17. *Piping, cording, and tucks. 1. With piping, cord is inserted in fabric. 2. Fold edge under the cord cut (see arrows). 3. Lapping method. 4. With tucks, snip to the mark (at arrow), press and stitch. 5. A grid of tucks. Make cardboard template for marking. 6. Push tucks in two directions.*

MAKING PIECED JACKETS AND COATS

■ Tucks, Piping and More

You now have tried making bias tubing. Let's see how else you can use it and briefly explore other favorite embellishment methods.

Piping

Piping is fabric cut on the bias, folded in half lengthwise, right sides out, and stitched with a ¼″ (6mm) seam. Piping on a jacket is shown in the color section. The jacket in Fig. 2-3 has piping without an inserted cord. You can buy piping but it must be prewashed. It's easy to make at home and the color will be just what you want.

Note: To preshrink purchased bias tape piping, cording, etc.: Leave the article on the card, soak a few minutes in hot water, remove from water, bend card, let dry, and press.

Using Fasturn is the easiest way to make piping with or without inserted cord. Use acrylic yarn for insertion because it won't shrink. Use one strand or more, depending on the look you want.

To insert cord without Fasturn, cut bias and fold together with right-sides-out. Lay the cord in the fold of the bias and, using a zipper foot, start sewing by stitching over the short end of the cord and bias to secure the cord. Try not to stretch bias as you sew. See Fig. 5-17, part 1.

Joining the piping is shown in Fig. 5-17, part 2. For a join like part 2, the neater of the two methods, leave 1″ (2.5cm) at either end with which to work. Pull out one side of the filler cord and cut so the ends will butt together. Rip a few stitches on one seam, fold the seam back to the inside, and slip over the other side. For a join like part 3, bring both ends of cording down across themselves and stitch.

Bias Tubing, Cording, or Soutache

In using tubing, cording, or soutache, the seam of the bias strip is on the inside, so the sewn tube must be reversed. This is easily done with

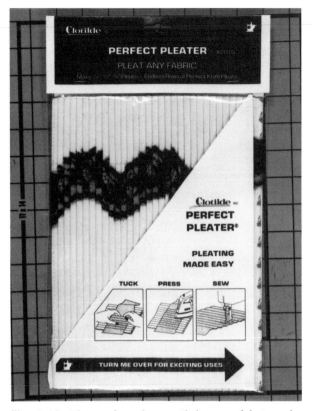

Fig. 5-18. *The Perfect Pleater. Slide your fabric to be pleated in the grooves of the pleater. Steam and let dry. Good directions come with the pleater. Available only at Clotilde's (listed in the Supply List).*

Fasturn, a bodkin, safety pin, or cord turner (the long metal wire with a hook on one end and a ring on the other). Sometimes the seam allowance is enough stuffing for the cord. If you want to add cord, using Fasturn is the easiest way. Or you can sew your bias over a length of cord twice as long as you need. Secure the cord to the bias in the center of the cord, sew and then turn bias back onto the other half of the cord. Cut off what isn't needed.

Your serger can make quick cording. Serge a chain as long as you want the cord to be. Bring the chain around to the front of the foot. Fold a bias strip lengthwise with right sides together and bring the chain around to the front and place inside the bias. Serge the raw edge of the bias without catching the chain inside. Reverse bias over the serged chain.

Cording or soutache looks great formed into designs and stitched to your garment. Many sewing machines have a cording foot that makes sewing cord on a flat surface easier. Cording is used for straps, frogs, cords for necklaces, and braiding for belts.

Finish the ends of cording like the first method in piping (see page 87) or hide the end under a cord and *secure firmly* with hand stitches.

Tucks

Tucks add texture, dimension, and visual interest. They can be small, made with a tucking foot on lightweight fabric. The smocking pleater and the Perfect Pleater (see Fig. 5-18) are aids in making tucks (see Supply List). Any section of your garment can have tucks added as with any other piecing. Some sewing stores offer a pleating service for a small fee. (See Sew Biz, listed in the Supply List.)

Make tucks by marking and sewing a piece of fabric. Cut small snips at the top and bottom of the fabric (see Fig. 5-17, part 4). Then press and sew the tucks. Using the machine quilting guide on your machine (see page 63) will help keep the tucking straight. For variety, your tucks can be random widths or lapped in a grid pattern as in Fig. 5-17, part 5. Make a cardboard template for marking the grid pattern. Tucks also can be sewn and twisted (see Fig. 5-17, part 6). You can add acrylic yarn or preshrunk cable cord inside the tuck to make it more prominent or use your twin needles stitched over cable cord underneath

for a tuck look. Experiment with tightening the top or bobbin tension for a more pronounced tuck. Tucks give you lots of possibilities for embellishment. The most beautiful variations are in Lois Ericson's book entitled *Tucks* (listed in the Bibliography).

Puffs

In *Wearable Art for Real People* (listed in the Bibliography), Mary Mashuta shows how to make puffed areas in square, rectangular, or triangular shapes to raise an area of your patchwork. The puff then can be tacked in the middle with a bead or button or stuffed with a bit of batting. The puffs are similar to the puff-quilting technique.

Free-Stitch Bonded Appliqué

See Jan Beaney's *The Art of the Needle* (listed in the Bibliography) and an article in *Bernina Magazine* (spring/summer, no. 14 [no year listed]) featuring a jacket designed by Alice Allen.

Free-stitch bonded appliqué features many textures and objects bonded to a base fabric and then decorated with free-machine stitching.

Supplies

☐ A base fabric as large as the garment you wish to make. Draw your pattern on the base fabric

Fig. 5-19. *Free-stitch bonded appliqué with an assortment of cotton fabric and threads and polyester batting. Now it is a vest, but I may add darker polyester fabric as sleeves and convert it to a blouse, with more lace added to the neckline.*

but do not cut it out yet. Start with a small project. If you intend to wash the garment, be sure everything used is preshrunk.

☐ A sheer fabric or net the same size as the base.

☐ Double-sided adhesive fabric such as Wonder Under or Stitch Witchery.

☐ An assortment of threads, yarns, sequins, ribbons, laces, ultra-suede scraps, fabric scraps, beads, and braids. Color-coordinate your "mess."

☐ An assortment of embroidery threads and cords that you can apply with the sewing machine.

☐ Protective material for the iron and stiffening material while free-stitching. See the following directions.

Directions

Lay out your base fabric on your work table and play with your mess, arranging it until you are pleased with your design. The arrangement can be representational or free-form. Cut small pieces of double-sided bonded fabric and place them under all the design pieces, two layers in thick places. Peel the paper backing off the Wonder Under before using.

The second step is bonding with your iron. Use typing paper, Easy Way Pressing Sheet, or Teflon Pressing Sheets (available through Perfect Notions) to prevent getting adhesive on your iron. Lay this material over the whole piece before bonding. Press.

Place Tear-A-Way, freezer paper, or batting behind your work and free-stitch with the feed dogs down in random patterns, using embroidery threads in your machine. Change thread colors frequently.

Either place net or sheer fabric over your work and continue stitching, or place no net and continue to stitch until everything is fastened down. Alice Allen ties her composition together with swirls of cording applied with a cording foot.

Another alternative is to use a sheer for the base and the top. The result will be a filmy, see-through fabric. When bonding with two sheers, the protective paper will need to be on the bottom as well as the top to protect the ironing board and the iron. Remember to use a stiffening paper when stitching the free-embroidery stitches. See Fig. 5-19.

■ More Ideas for Embellishments

1. Appliqué is made so much more easily with a fusible paper-backed webbing like Wonder Under. Good directions are on the wrapper.

2. Machine or hand embroidery.

3. Smocking by hand or machine.

4. Cross-stitch by hand or over the needlework by machine (see Fig. 5-20). The over the needlework method uses cross-stitch patterns, colored threads and tiny needles that are 6″ (15cm) long. Your pattern is under the needles on paper. Designs can be as intricate as any hand cross-stitch technique. Any zigzag machine can stitch over the needles. See your sewing machine dealer for further instructions. Kits for practice are available from Treadleart (listed in the Supply List).

5. Added laces, ribbon, and other fancy trims.

6. Trapunto by hand or machine-dense stitching in large or small areas (see Chapter 6).

7. Hand-painted and dyeing techniques. Dyeing gives your fabrics a softer feel than painting.

8. Machine-made medallions or Battenberg lace. See the *Know Your Machine* series of books from Chilton Book Company and the book on machine embroidery by Robbie Fanning.

9. Tassels, store-bought or handmade buttons, or mirrors can be added. See *Sewing It Yourself* by Lois Ericson and Diane Frode (listed in the Bibliography).

10. Lettering, either by hand or machine.

See the Bibliography for help in these methods. Add to this list as you discover new ideas. You may want to jot ideas on a piece of paper and use it as a bookmark while you read this book.

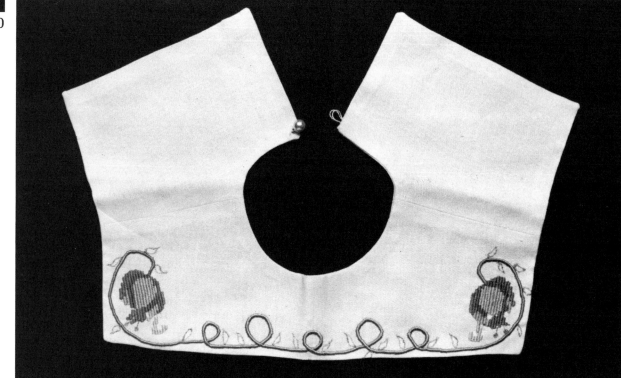

Fig. 5-20. *Cross-stitched collar with stitching over the needle. Made of linen fabric with Sulky (rayon embroidery) thread.*

■ ■ ■

PART III

CONSTRUCTING QUILTED JACKETS

CHAPTER 6

■ ■ ■

Densely Quilted Jackets

One of my favorite quilting techniques is dense quilting, which means to free-quilt the background of a piece, causing the design shapes to pop out. I have developed the technique, but I didn't invent it.

Years ago I tried to shade a fabric collage piece using the bare needle of the sewing machine with the feed dogs down. The thread kept breaking and that project ended up in the trash.

I bought place mats in Pittsburgh made by Tobey Wolken, with charming vegetables as the design. They were made with the machine free (feed dogs down), which sparked my interest once again. As a result I attended a class in trapunto taught by Barbara Brackman at the North Carolina Quilt Symposium.

I had seen and admired Elizabeth Gurrier's humorous white, three-dimensional angel and bed scenes.

While taking a Procion dyeing class at Arrowmont with Lenore Davis, I was shown how to set my thirty-year-old Singer machine for free quilting. It was there I learned to use the darning foot to prevent thread breaking. Lenora free-stitches scallops on her dyed cotton velveteen wall hangings. Sewing the scallops actually quilts the pieces.

Next, I learned machine embroidery, Battenberg lace, and other dense-quilting techniques, but found the use of the hoop needed in these methods confining.

After learning to paint fabric with dye to use in making garments, I wanted a freer method to quilt them, more in character with the loose designs I was painting. I started free-quilting lines 2″–3″ (5cm–7.5cm) apart and drawing small figures with the machine. See the color section. The batting in the sandwich gave enough stiffness so that a hoop was not needed.

McFarland design from a piece of embroidered linen inherited from my aunt, Margaret McFarland.

As I learned more about quilting, I found that seed stitching and outlining stitch techniques helped to push the background down, making the design area pop up.

The last discovery was to free-stitch rows of machine stitches much closer than before ($\frac{1}{4}''$ [6mm]) to puff up the design area.

I hope you will enjoy the process as much as I have. We'll start by making some practice pieces (see Figs. 6-4, 6-5, 6-6, and 6-11).

■ Getting Started

The best way to learn to dense-quilt is to get out some old muslin and make practice pieces. Your skill with the method will develop with practice.

Get out your machine instruction book and look up darning or machine embroidery. Set your machine as directed. Any brand of sewing machine can darn *except* the Singer Featherweight—and I may stand corrected about that.

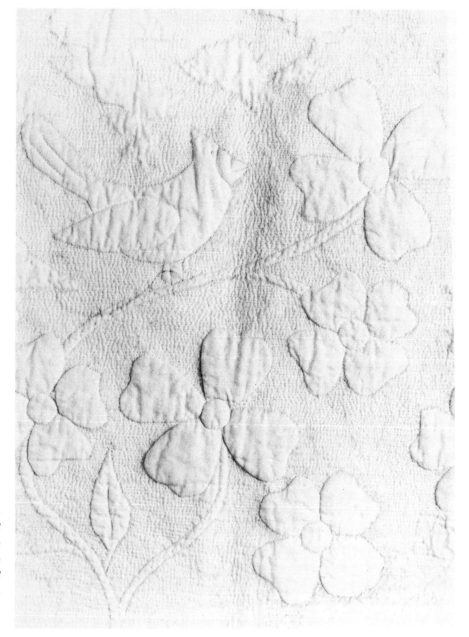

Fig. 6-1. *Marie Wood's 100-percent cotton dense-quilted vest of her own design using the North Carolina state flower (dogwood) and bird (cardinal). Vest uses horizontal dense machine stitch. 1985.*

Darning involves lowering or covering the feed dogs so the fabric can be pushed in any direction while stitching. If your thread cutter is on the machine's base, cover it with masking tape.

Remove your presser foot and attach the darning foot (called a "hopper foot" in Raleigh) or spring. My experience is that the spring does not work as well as the darning foot. See drawings of various feet in Fig. 6-2. A darning foot looks like a tiny hoop. It fits slanted, short, and long shank machines. The Elna foot will fit all short-shank domestic machines and the others can be found in sewing-machine repair shops where there

is a catalog for ordering parts. (See the Bibliography for a source.) For better visibility, some darning feet are made of plastic or have the front of the hoop cut out. I have known students who cut out and smoothed the fronts themselves.

A brand new spring needle is on the market made by Elna. It is a needle with a spring wrapped around it and a tiny disk at the bottom that helps with stitch formation. The needle can replace your darning foot. It will be great for those sewing machines that darning feet don't fit well. The needle can be used for any free stitching, but I think it works best when the work is in a hoop. You can

**Machine Quilting
and Darning Feet**

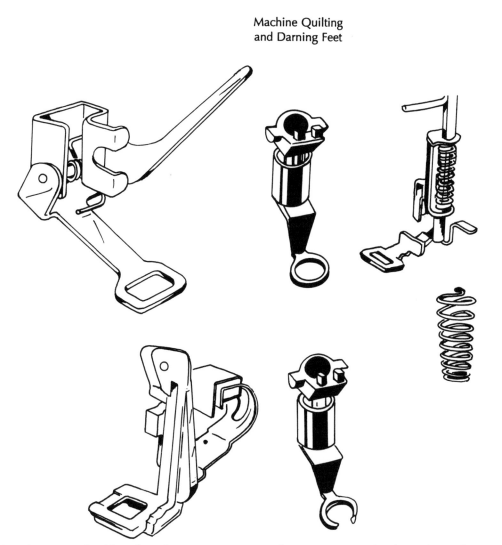

Fig. 6-2. *Darning or embroidery feet. See your sewing machine instruction book or dealer for the type to fit your machine. See the Supply List for sources.*

DENSELY QUILTED JACKETS

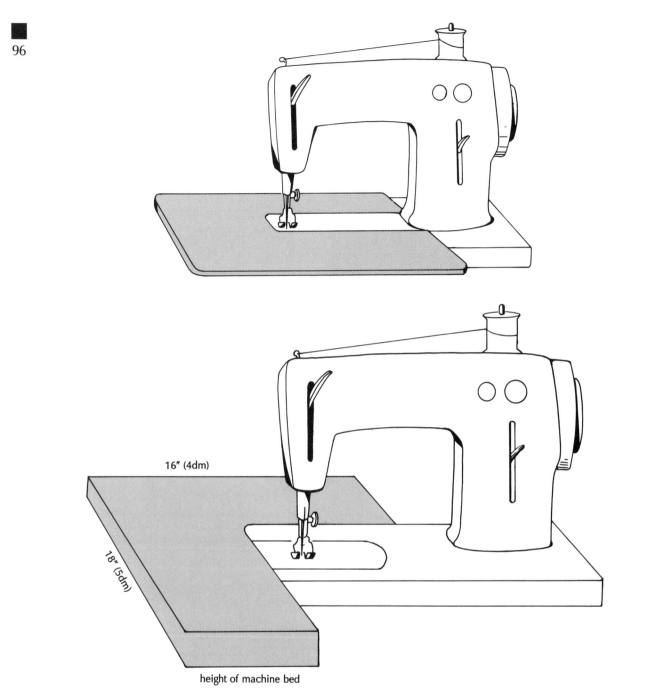

16″ (4dm)

18″ (5dm)

height of machine bed

Fig. 6-3. *Machine extensions. 1. Commercial. Each machine company has a slightly different design. Extensions come with some machines or can be ordered. 2. Homemade. Some type of extension really is a must for sewing with the feed dogs down to allow your hands to rest comfortably on the bed of the machine. Your machine set in a cabinet accomplishes the same thing. This one is made of heavy plywood covered with formica. The extension pushes up to machine and is not fastened. Designed and made by Marvin Spencer.*

see every stitch you make. Don't be intimidated by the distance between the needle and your work. Lower the presser foot and go ahead and stitch.

Be sure your machine is oiled and free of lint. Fill lots of bobbins. Use a new size 80/12 or 90/14 needle and polyester-wrapped thread in the color of your fabric (see hints on thread in Chapter 1's Shopping List). Set the stitch length and width at 0 or however your manual directs.

If your machine has a needle-down position, use it. Set your machine on a table or in its extension bed. It is helpful to have room to position your hands while stitching. See Fig. 6-3, which shows both commercial and homemade extensions. Your hands are flat on either side of the needle. Arms are bent at the elbow, and the bed of the machine is best placed at the same height as your elbow. I hope you have found an adjustable chair to use at your machine. I have brightened my chair, which came from an office supply company, with fabric covers.

Making a Fabric Sandwich

Enclose a piece of bonded polyester batting with fabric about 14″ (3.5dm) square. Use quilt-weight or extra-loft batting for good effects. A backing fabric is not essential but makes the work feel better and the construction easier. Pin the outside edges of your sandwich 4″ (1dm) apart. No basting is necessary.

Lower the presser foot. Take one stitch, holding onto the top thread, and pull the bobbin thread up. Pull the fabric hard while pushing hard on the foot pedal. See what a long stitch you can make? Do not pull the fabric, but push on the foot pedal. Look at the knot formed on the back— just like setting your stitch length at zero. Stitch side to side and up and down. It's just like drawing with charcoal on paper. In this case your hand and foot are controlling the machine. Think of yourself as a great fiber artist and visualize your name. Write it with the machine. Now you have an easy way to sign all of your work.

> **Hint:** Hold a wide piece of twill tape in a hoop with a backing fabric. Sign your name and date. Use the tape as a label in the garment.

Practice rows of free stitches about 3″ (7.5cm) apart. See Figs. 6-4 and 6-5. Start in the top middle of your practice piece and work all the way from top to bottom of your fabric. Always work from the center out and from a previous row of stitches out to prevent puckers on the front. Free stitches are very difficult to rip out. If you must rip, get in between the layers to make it easier. These stitches are useful in quilting garments and household items. Play and invent some new stitches on your practice piece.

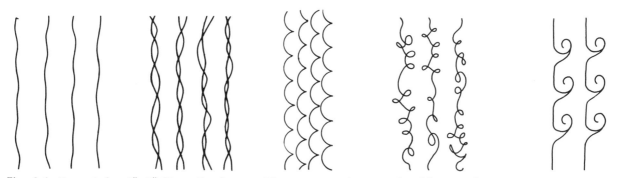

Fig. 6-4. Free stitches 2″–3″ (5cm–7cm) apart. These are not dense stitches. These stitches are a precursor to the dense machine stitching and are useful in themselves. By playing with your machine with the feed dogs down, you develop more such stitches.

■ ■ Dense Stitches

See Fig. 6-11, which shows a dense-stitch sampler. Draw four flower forms on a practice piece. Outline the flower forms with your free stitching. This is called "setting" the design. The area around each flower will be filled with different dense stitches.

Squiggle

See Fig. 6-6, part 1. Visualize following the shapes of a jigsaw puzzle and stitch. Keep stitches about ⅛″ (3mm) apart. Start right at the flower edge. Work from the center outward. With practice you can keep the foot pedal and your hands moving the fabric at a consistent pace, your "sig-

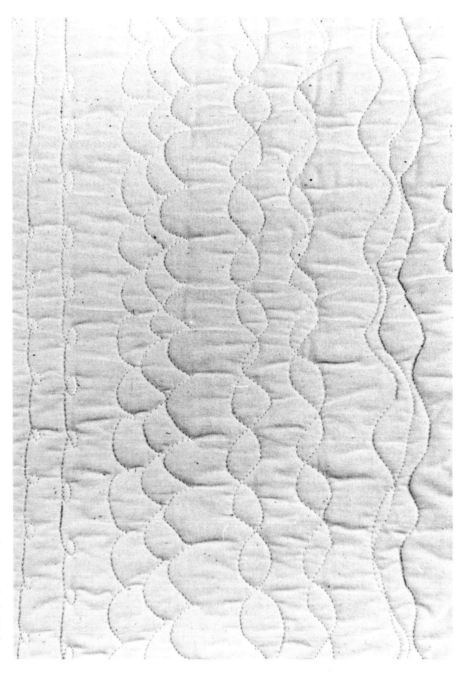

Fig. 6-5. *Sampler of three stitches 3″ (7.5cm) apart. These are not dense stitches, but are stitches I used first in machine quilting. These stitch patterns are very useful in designing. Make up more rows to add to your sampler.*

■
■
■ **CONSTRUCTING QUILTED JACKETS**

nature." Relax: This is fun. Stitches don't have to be the same length.

The key to doing the squiggle well is to vary the pattern as you sew. Make small circles as well as jigsaw cutout shapes. The squiggle looks best when the main design is simple, for it is a "busy" stitch.

Outline

See Fig. 6-6, part 2. Stitch $\frac{1}{8}''$ (3mm) around the flower and continue going around and around. You can use the inside or outside of the presser foot as a guide. When stopping in one area and going to the next, raise the needle to the up position and pull the work to where you want to go. There is no need to cut the thread and start again. Neither is there reason to clip the threads on the back. The outline stitch is difficult to do evenly, but don't worry about it if it looks like waves or echoes. If your design has stem lines, they need to be widened in order to show up or they'll be hidden in the dense background stitches. Make stem lines at least double the dimension between the dense stitches.

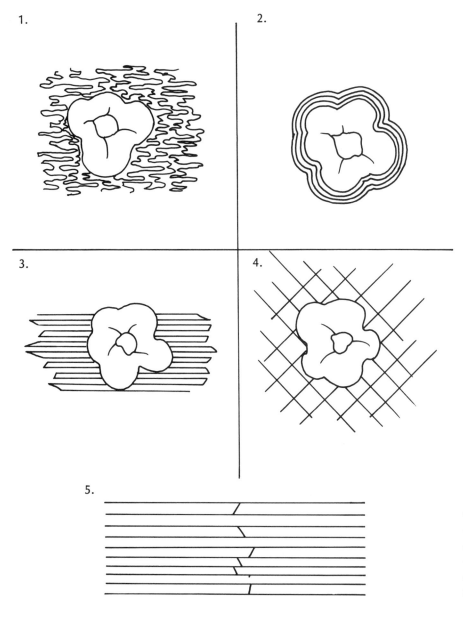

1.

2.

3.

4.

5.

Fig. 6-6. *Dense stitches: 1) squiggle, 2) outline, 3) horizontal, 4) crosshatch, and 5) an example of how to stagger long lines of horizontal stitching to avoid a ridge.*

DENSELY QUILTED JACKETS

Horizontal

See Fig. 6-6, part 3. This is probably the most effective stitch for bringing up your designs. Do not draw all the lines. Just draw some guidelines about 5″ (12.5cm) apart with your purple disappearing pencil to give your eye something to follow. The grain of the fabric also helps keep you straight. Starting at one edge of the flower, pull fabric away from the flower in a straight line, come to the end, make a bar or slant line, and come back to the flower about ¼″ (6mm) away. To get to the next line, travel on the "set" line of the flower. Work by pulling the fabric toward you and back, not side to side, which is harder to get straight. Continue in this manner until all the area around the flower is punched down. Stagger the slant lines at the end of each line of stitching. Later you can start other rows of stitches here and they will blend in if the line is staggered. See Fig. 6-6, part 5.

With the horizontal stitch, 5″ (12.5cm) is as long as you can comfortably make a row and make it straight. Beyond that you must move your hands, and then the stitch begins to wiggle. Needle-down helps and you will get steadier with practice. This stitch looks good placed vertically, as well as horizontally, on a garment.

Hint: It is not necessary to carry the horizontal stitch to the edge of a garment. Vary the ending of your rows, and when the side seams are sewn together there will be another design.

Crosshatch

See Fig. 6-6, part 4. Sew diagonal lines ½″ (1.3cm) apart starting on a set line. Draw the first line to get your angle. I usually draw a diagonal line through the design. Stitch over the first set of stitched lines at a right angle ½″ (1.3cm) apart.

Practice the four dense stitches until you find your favorite.

Hints: See Fig. 6-1 of Marie Wood's vest.

1. Rotate your work in the machine when you can't see the design anymore. Turn the fabric

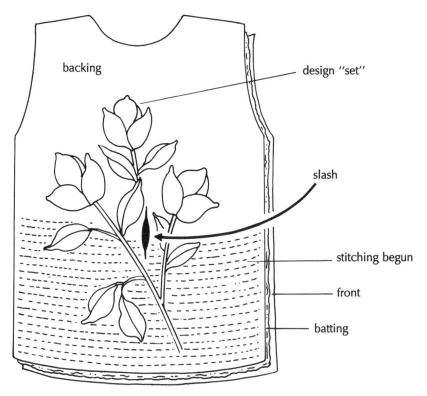

Fig. 6-7. *Slitting the backing of your sandwich to relieve a potential pucker on the front. Determine the direction of the pull on the front and carefully cut the backing until the pucker is relieved. This is a great help.*

backing

design "set"

slash

stitching begun

front

batting

CONSTRUCTING QUILTED JACKETS

with the needle in the down position. It usually is not necessary to raise the presser foot.

2. When stopping the machine while setting or working dense stitches, leave the needle in the down position or you will have an unwanted zig-zag.

3. If an area looks like it will pucker, take your work out of the machine and slit the backing in the pucker area. Voilà! With a little pulling on the front, you will have no pucker. See Fig 6-7. Once in a great while, I have to put the area in a hoop to keep it pulled tight and smooth.

4. Use the power of visualization. Picturing the shape you want and the direction you will go before you stitch can improve your work. Practice relaxing your hands, neck, and feet. Let your experience with this method come from the right (or creative) side of your brain.

5. If you are making a small item such as a cosmetic case, draw your design on a larger piece of fabric and don't cut it out until the dense stitching is finished. Then trim to size. You can't easily hold on to a small piece of fabric and keep control.

6. If your thread keeps breaking, change the needle. We tend to pull too hard as we are learning and bend needles as a result.

7. If you find your stitches are too long, push harder on the foot pedal. Run the machine faster, but don't pull the fabric any more than normal.

8. When moving the needle and shifting to another place, pull enough top thread out behind the needle to prevent snagging. If a snag occurs, check the bobbin case for thread wrapped around it.

■ Variations

Use colored fabric. Light colors work best. Polished cottons work well, but don't expect all of the sheen to remain after the fabric is washed. Rayon embroidery thread is good for a dressier look. Match your thread to your fabric carefully. I stitched a dusty rose jacket with thread that was too light and it looks messy.

A black drapery fabric with lots of polish (made with resin) makes a nice garment. See Fig. 6-8. You do not want to spend hours making the jacket

Fig. 6-8. *Black tunic with design that was taken from a piece of weaving that looked organic. Vertical rows of sample dense machine stitches are surrounded by curved lines. Fabric composition is unknown, except that it is a highly glazed drapery fabric. 1988. Owner: Anita J. Clowdis.*

and not have satisfying results to show for it, so choose the fabric and thread color carefully. All the pieces I did in the beginning were of muslin. I loved the contrast of a utilitarian fabric made into something beautiful.

Use colored threads for an interesting look. For a heavier look on the front, wind bobbins with embroidery floss, draw your design on the underside, and stitch from the underside. You will need to pull the floss threads to the back and tie or secure with Fray Check.

Add extra scraps of batting to an area you want to emphasize. Just pin the batting in place and set as usual. On a garment, watch where you place extra batting. Thickening some body areas is not flattering.

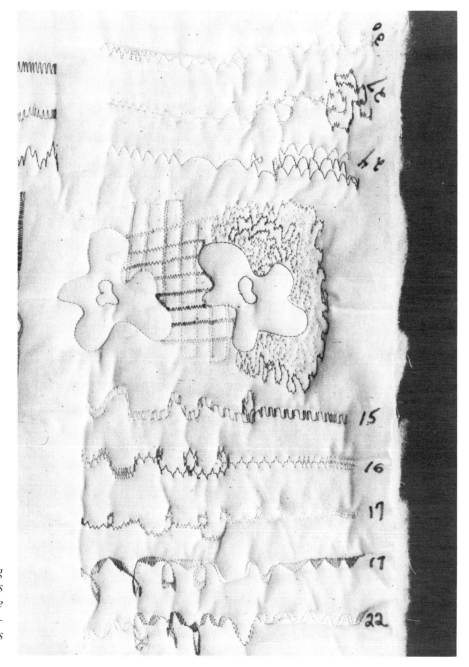

Fig. 6-9. *Sampler of zigzag and programmed stitches with feed dogs down. The numbers refer to the numbers of programmed stitches on a Bernina 1130.*

CONSTRUCTING QUILTED JACKETS

Fig. 6-10. *A blackbird with dense machine stitches completed and ready to be sewn into a tote.*

Fig. 6-11. *Sampler with four dense machine stitches: horizontal, outline, squiggle, and crosshatch. Can you see that the stitches are not the same length?*

DENSELY QUILTED JACKETS

Hint: Save all your batting scraps for the day you will want to make a stuffed animal or doll. Keep a plastic bag hanging on your work table for batting scraps, as well as a bag for trash. I even have a third bag for small pieces of cotton which I will use in scrap quilts. This is sorted by color a few times a year and stored in boxes.

Use two layers of batting throughout or extra-loft batting for warmth and extra puffiness. Cut extra batting from seam allowances to make seaming easier.

I do not try to match dense machine-quilt stitching on side seams or on shoulders because I like the variations in pattern (and it's impossible to match).

Make a sampler using the zigzag stitch with your sewing machine in the free mode. Try using your programmed stitches. You can get some interesting results. See Fig. 6-9.

Another stitch you can use on your dense pieces for flower centers or larger areas is the French knot worked by machine. With your machine set free and using straight stitch, sew around and around in a small area. Lift the presser foot and move to the next area where you want a French knot and repeat.

Wonderful things happen with free (not dense) stitches on cotton velveteen. Try making a bunch of grapes and see what wonderful puffs or circles you get.

The idea is to play and have fun with the method. I would love to hear about any new discoveries you make.

■ Construction

The densely quilted jacket is constructed differently from the plain and pieced jackets because it is necessary to cover the messy back of dense stitching. See Fig. 6-17.

Shopping List

☐ 2-½ yds. (2.2m) of 100-percent cotton permanent-press muslin for the outer shell of jacket (more if size 16 or larger). Cotton and polyester blends will work. I have used some *Polished Apple* brand fabric but the sheen does not survive washing. Preshrink all fabrics.

☐ 2-½ yds. (2.2m) polyester-bonded batting of quilt weight (see Chapter 2 Shopping List).

☐ 2-½ yds. (2.2m) inner lining (backing) (see Chapter 2 Shopping List).

☐ 3 yds. (2.7m) fabric of similar weight for lining and bias trim. The fabric for the lining can be lining fabric if slipping into the jacket easily is important to you. I use lining fabric sometimes but I personally prefer to keep the entire garment cotton.

☐ Pattern: a commercial jacket pattern that is straight, boxy with no darts, and has set-in sleeves. Buy a size ample for you. Recently I have been using Butterick 5575 (which has an ample sleeve), but each pattern company has a similiar pattern.

☐ Marking equipment includes a blue washable pen or a purple disappearing pencil.

☐ Thread to match the outer shell.

☐ Large sheet of light-colored paper or grafted-pattern fabric such as Stacy Pattern Tracer for your design. Brown paper (paper bags) will not work.

☐ Black permanent marking pen.

☐ Sewing machine in good order, with a darning (embroidery) foot or spring.

Cutting

Disregard all facings and interfacings in your pattern. Make any necessary alterations. Cut two fronts, a back, and two sleeves from outer shell

Fig. 6-12. *Vest with the Amy amaryllis dense machine design of 100-percent cotton, using a horizontal dense machine stitch. Amy is an amaryllis that bloomed at my farm in Virginia in the middle of a snowstorm. Drawn by Ruth Steinberger. 1989.*

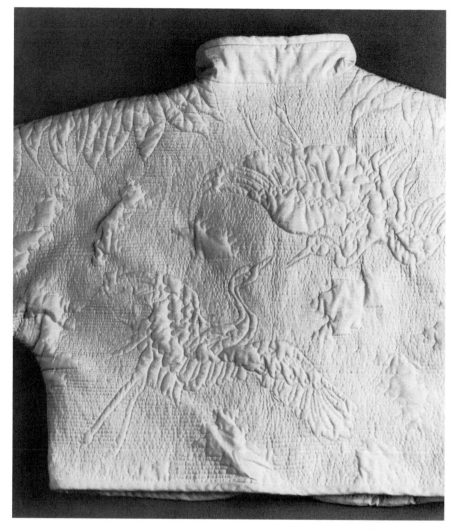

Fig. 6-13. *Back of 100-percent cotton cranes design dense jacket—my most popular design. Taken from an Oriental drawing that was about 5" (12.5cm) square. Cranes are a fertility symbol in China. I can't bear to make another one. 1986. Owner: my daughter-in-law, Sheila Moore.*

fabric, leaving an extra $\frac{1}{2}''$ (1.3cm) all around for fabric shrinkage from quilting. We will make adjustments later. Using your outer shell pieces as a pattern and then cut the batting and inner lining (backing). Do *not* cut the lining at this time. Mark center sleeve and sleeve notches. Press fabric of outer shell.

Design

Cut paper or fabric pattern material the size of the five pattern pieces. Arrange your design in a pleasing manner. See Chapter 7 on design. Look at your design as if it were in black and white;

the black area is the part to be pushed down by quilting and the white area will remain puffed up. Keep your design simple and not too small. Widen any stem lines so they won't be lost by the background stitches. Outline the design on paper with the black permanent marking pen. Lay your outer shell pieces over the paper pattern and trace the design, using the blue or purple pen. If you can't see the paper pattern to trace because your fabric is dark and not see-through, cut templates of the main design pieces. See Fig. 6-15 for sample templates. Arrange the templates on the garment pieces and draw around them. Add connecting lines. A ruler or flexible ruler helps here.

Fig. 6-14. *Rose design set in a medallion on the back of a jacket. The design was drawn from pictures in a plant nursery catalog. Setting in a medallion, oval, circle, (I used the lid of a canner to draw the circle), or design set in square on point can save you some dense stitching. Double your line of the medallion and use a less-dense stitch outside of the medallion. On this jacket I stitched a big crosshatch with the feed dogs up and used the quilt guide. I set the stitch length at 0 to fasten thread at the beginning of every line. 1985.*

Fig. 6-15. *Templates for dense machine-quilting patterns. These templates are for the all-over pattern. It is useful to make templates of your favorite designs to arrange the design elements as you prefer.*

CONSTRUCTING QUILTED JACKETS

Hint: If I plan enough time to draw and "set" at one time, I like to use the purple disappearing pencil. This eliminates the wash-out step of the blue wash-out pen. I can go back and stitch the background when I have smaller amounts of time.

Notice that in the photographs some of the designs are set in medallions, circles, ovals, or squares set on point. Fewer dense stitches are required outside these design areas. This saves time and gives a nice contrast. See Fig. 6-16.

You can lay your paper pattern directly over the jacket, pin, and set by stitching through paper and sandwich. Then tear away the paper. Marking is eliminated. I've done this in machine embroidery and used the idea on the wool cape. It is hard to get the paper out without pulling stitches. You also can't use the design again without retracing it.

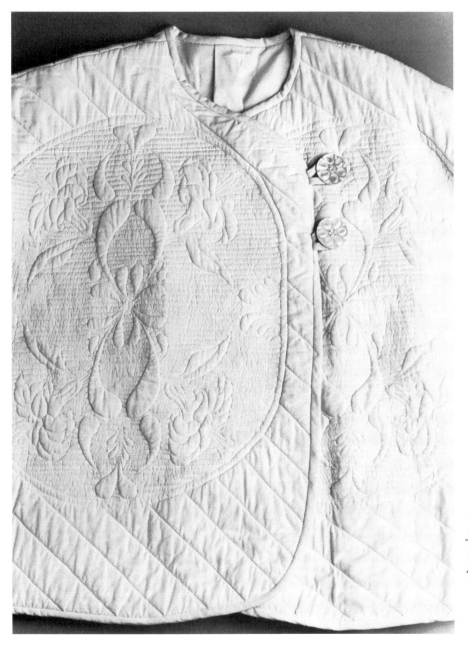

Fig. 6-16. *Symmetrical day lily design jacket. The idea for this design came from a quilting pattern that had pieced flowers where I placed the day lily. The design is set in a medallion with diagonal lines outside the medallion. 1985.*

DENSELY QUILTED JACKETS

■ Sandwich

Make five fabric sandwiches for your pattern pieces with backing on the bottom; batting next; and outer shell, right-side-up, last. Pin outside edges every 4″ (1dm). Check to be sure you have reversed one sleeve and one front piece.

"Set" your design, starting in the middle (review general machine-quilting rules in Chapter 4). See Fig. 6-17. Stitch the background with the

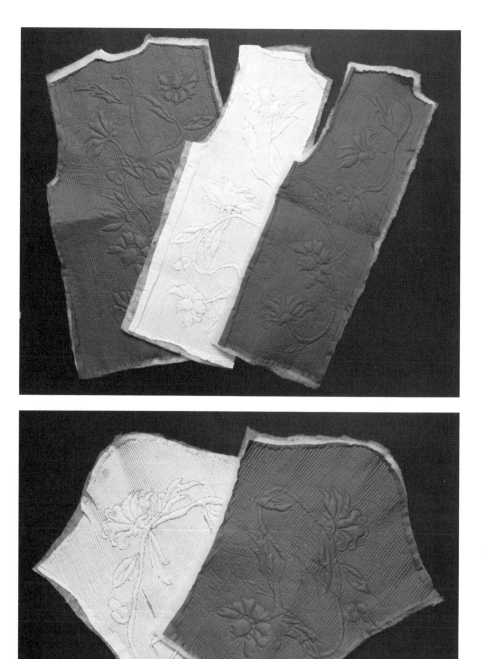

Fig. 6-17. *Five densely machine-quilted sandwiches ready to be assembled into a jacket. This is a McFarland design.*

CONSTRUCTING QUILTED JACKETS

type of stitch you have chosen. The quilting of the five pieces will take about five hours.

Trimming, Fitting, and Lining

As you quilt, the batting flattens and works out of the sandwich. If your batting and inner lining are protruding, trim them to the outer shell on all five pieces. Pin shoulder and side seams. Try on for size. Adjust. Check the length of the sleeves. Make sure that the front side seams and side seams of the back are the same length. Round the corners of the jacket front center, bottom, and upper center edges (if you are not adding a collar).

Fold completed pieces in half and lay them on the lining folded in half. Cut lining pieces, following size of adjusted sandwiches, and allow an extra 2″ (5cm) at top center back, slanting to nothing at the jacket back bottom. See Fig. 6-19. This extra is used later to form a pleat, giving ease across the shoulders.

Sewing Order

Stitch shoulder seams; press open lightly. Pin seams in open position at edges. Repeat with the lining.

On sleeves, run two rows of gathering stitches between notches over cap. Pin the sleeve to the jacket, matching center sleeve seam with the shoulder seam. Adjust the ease. Stitch from the sleeve side. Check the outside for a smooth finish. If there are no puckers, stitch a second time $\frac{1}{4}$″

Fig. 6-18. *Vest of 100-percent cotton with Pennsylvania Dutch design set in square on point. This design is simple enough to use the squiggle dense machine stitch. 1990.*

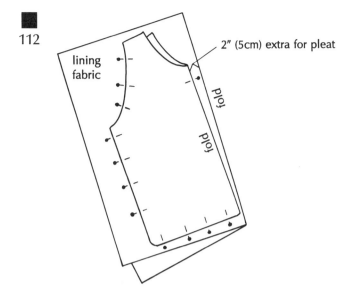

Fig. 6-19. *Cutting the back lining. As shown, the completed back sandwich is folded in half. I used to form a pleat all the way down the back until a student showed me this method of slanting the back.*

(6mm) away from previous stitching. Trim the seam. Push the seam toward the sleeve. Repeat with lining; you will be able to press lining seams.

Stitch long seam of the underarm and side seam, matching underarm seam carefully. Sew slowly in this thick area. You may want to stitch the underarm seam twice. Pin seams open at the bottom of the sleeve and the bottom of the side seam. Repeat with the lining. Press the lining seams open.

Refer to page 28 in Chapter 2 if using a collar, fasteners, or adding bias binding. To make a pocket for the inside of the jacket: fold a 10″ × 5″ (2.5dm × 1.2dm) piece of lining fabric right sides together. Stitch sides, trim, and reverse. Sew by machine to lining only.

Insert lining into the jacket, wrong sides together. Pin at all seams. Form a pleat at the top center back. Pin. See Fig. 6-20 and instructions for finishing the neck edge.

You can continue to enjoy your jacket by washing it on a cool, delicate machine setting. Machine-dry on cool delicate or line-dry. Shake to fluff. Do not iron.

■ Designs for Dense Machine Quilting

The designs shown in Figs. 6-21 through 6-29 are designs used on garments in this book. They are presented to help get you started in dense machine stitching. Throughout the book, especially at the beginning of each book part, are more designs that can be adapted.

To use these designs you will need to do one of two things. First, you may have access to an enlarging photocopier (found in print shops). On paper, trace the design out of the book using a black pen or marker. Take that to the print shop for photocopying. Having the design enlarged

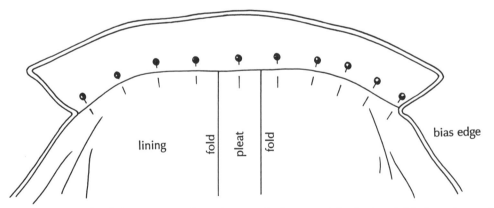

Fig. 6-20. *Pleat in the top back lining pinned in place, with the top of the lining folded under and ready for hand stitching. In the dense machine-quilted jacket, the neckline of the lining is staystitched. Clip to the staystitching, fold under, and hand-stitch to the collar/neck edge to form the pleat as you pin and stitch.*

Fig. 6-21. *Trellis design.*

twice will give you an area of about 32″ × 45″ (8dm × 1.2m). You may end up with three or four pieces of paper to tape together for your jacket back. Or, once the design elements are enlarged, cut out design elements (flowers, leaves, etc.) and arrange them on a paper or fabric copy of the back. Add stem lines, enclose in a circle, etc. Fronts can repeat the back and sleeves can take part of the design. I make the design for the back only and use parts of it on the sleeves and front.

The second way to enlarge the designs is to graph the design. On paper, trace the design from the book. Find the middle by folding your paper. Find the middle of the jacket back on the paper pattern. Draw a grid on each using a yardstick on the back piece. Copy the design from the smaller drawing to the larger using one-half, one-quarter, etc. lines. Go over the design lines with the black marker. Remember to save any design work you do.

Feel free to use the designs in other ways: appliqué, machine embroidery, cross stitch, or whatever interests you. You can have the designs shrunk as well as enlarged at the print shop. See Figs. 6-21 through 6-28.

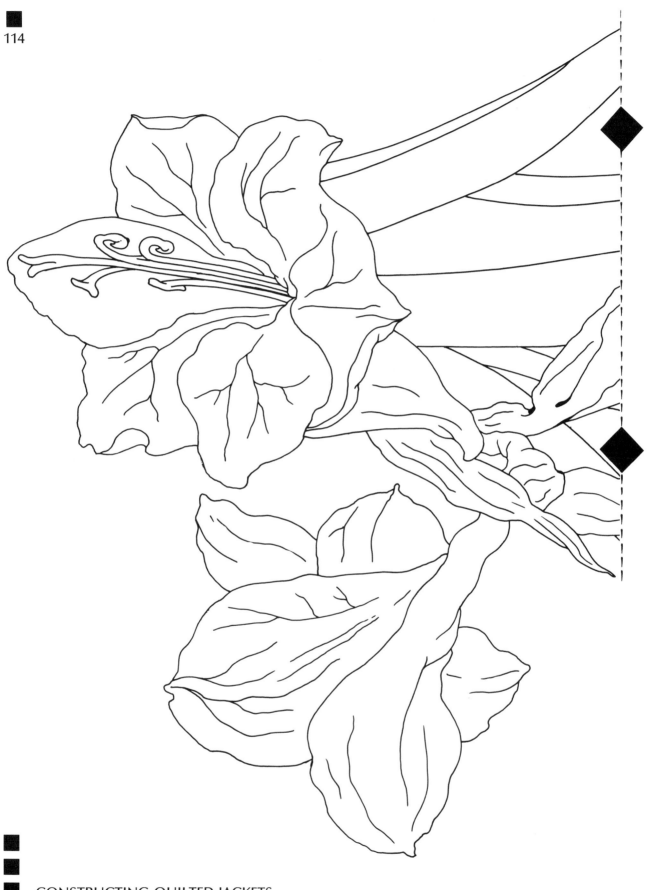

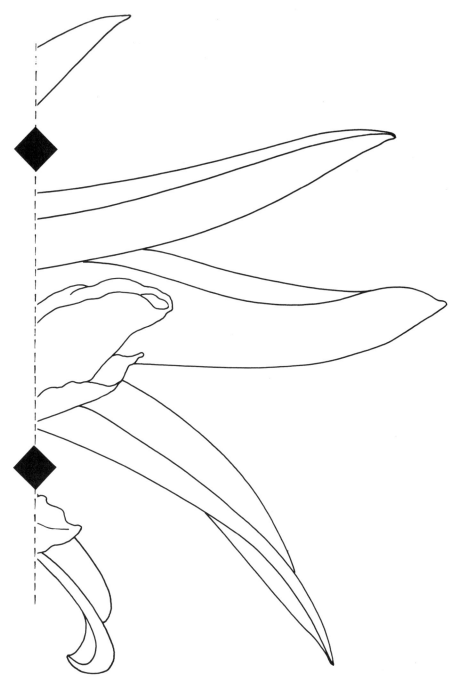

Fig. 6-22. *Amy amaryllis design.*

Fig. 6-23. *All-over design.*

Fig. 6-24. *Cranes design.*

CONSTRUCTING QUILTED JACKETS

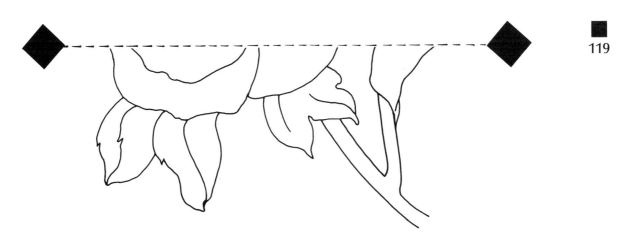

Fig. 6-25. *Rose design.*

Fig. 6-26. *Paisley design.*

DENSELY QUILTED JACKETS

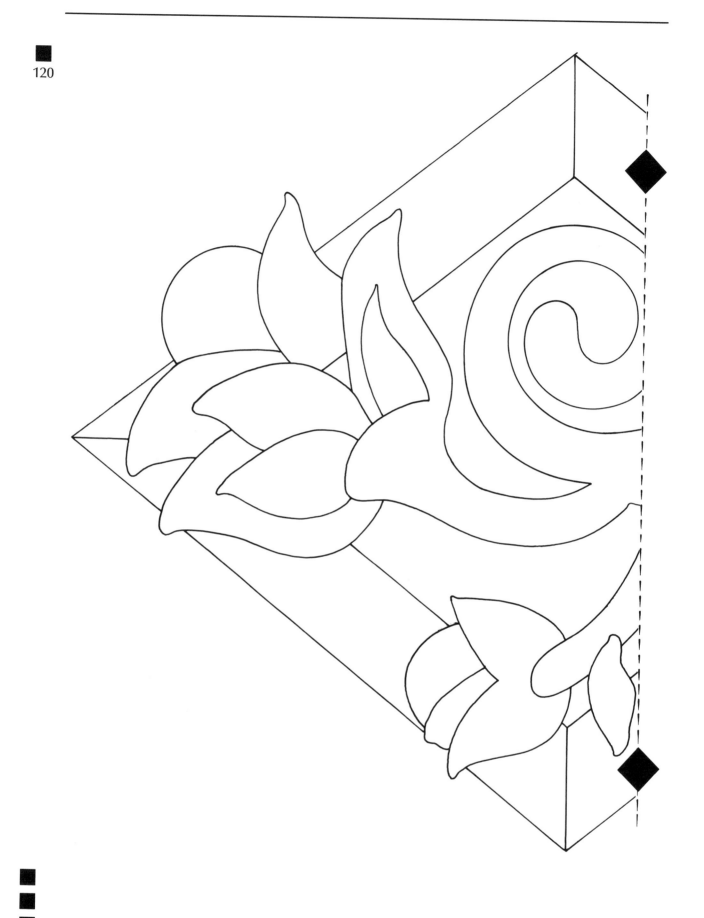

Fig. 6-27. *Pennsylvania Dutch design.*

Fig. 6-28. *Symmetrical day lily design.*

Fig. 6-29. *Art Nouveau dense machine-quilting design.*

■ Dense Machine Quilting on Other Fabrics

Here are my findings working with different fabrics and the dense machine-stitching technique.

Polyester Satin Robe

The robe shown in Fig. 6-30 has dense machine quilting part way down the front and around the collar. Dense machine stitching is also on both sides of the lapels so that the design shows when they are turned back. There is a layer of batting in the design areas and Sulky thread (rayon embroidery) was used in a matching color.

I'm pleased with the look, but not the fabric. I find polyester hard and unforgiving. If I repeat the project, it will be in cotton sateen. Cotton sateen dyes beautifully and feels good.

Silk Jumpsuit and Jacket

A photograph in the color section shows a silk jacket. The pattern used for the jacket was Easy McCalls 4741 offered by *Sew News*. The sleeve comes in two pieces. I sewed the two pieces together *except* the top 5″ (1.2dm) before cutting the batting and backing. The joining of the sleeves gave me a flat piece on which to quilt. The design was my mother's from the 1920s, when she was a student at Carnegie Tech. I used three spools of Sulky thread. It was stuffed with regular batting and an old sheet was used as backing. Another time I may use a rayon backing to make the whole garment softer.

Before sewing with silk I reviewed *Sensa-*

Fig. 6-30. *Polyester satin robe with the design stitched in rayon thread. The design was adapted from a Japanese motif in a Dover design book (see the Bibliography). Batting in the collar, lapels, and tie belt only. 1990.*

tional Silk (listed in the Bibliography). Use sharper, smaller pins and pin only in the seam allowances. Silk seems to be alive and wants to move. Marking was difficult and in places was more easily done with dots instead of lines. I used the purple pen.

I'm pleased with the results and will work with silk and dense machine stitching again.

Wool Cape

This is the cape for those of you who like a warm neck and shoulders. See the color section. Easy McCalls 3934 pattern was used with 100-percent wool. The pattern does not call for a lining but does serge the edges with fancy thread. After quilting the wool plus batting and backing, I cut a lining, sewed around three sides, and reversed it like a pillow case. Then I top-stitched the edges.

The design came from two sources. The first is a book called *Enticements* by Bill Tice (listed in the Bibliography). He used a curved edge and two types of quilting on one of his lounging outfits. The Celtic design came from *Celtic Quilt Designs* (listed in the Bibliography). The Celtic design had narrow lines, and I stitched over paper patterns to set them. I also used double batting behind the circular designs, which I discovered was unnecessary. If I were to sew the project again, I would use a free-flowing design, not a symmetrical design, that could be drawn easily on the area. I might use real trapunto (sew the lines and thread them from behind with acrylic thread). I went back to the Celtic design and satin-stitched over it. This is how I learn from doing.

The straight lines were quilted with the even-feed foot and feed dogs up. I used my homemade paper guide on the even-feed foot and it worked well. I tried stitching the outline stitch with the feed dogs down and it was so messy that I ripped out the stitches, then used the even-feed foot and the feed dogs up. The cape was bulky to handle, like a quilt. I rolled and pinned sections of it to make it easier to handle. The wool feels great and it is so forgiving.

I hope my experiments will help you avoid my mistakes.

For other examples of dense machine quilting projects, see the color section.

PART IV

■ ■ ■

CREATING YOUR OWN DESIGNS

CHAPTER 7

■ ■ ■

Off on Your Own

■ Design Principles

Learning to design is a satisfaction which will add a rich dimension to your life, a dimension that keeps on growing as you practice. What is really happening is you are learning to see well—learning to discern shapes and space, learning what pleases you and what doesn't. There are many ways to go about the process. Drawing classes are the most satisfying for me. I can be totally absorbed; using charcoal or a pencil, seeing the real shape and the commonality of shapes for the first time. The world could end and I would not know it. The time in drawing class is valuable both for allowing me to get away from the usual daily hassles and for learning new techniques. Design classes offered by colleges do a great job. A photography class gave me some good tips and helped develop my ability to really see what I'm looking at. Landscaping did the same. Perhaps you are a flower arranger and have learned ideas of design. I hope you experience some of these routes for yourself—*new* routes, so you will find your own vision and not copy that of others. See Nancy Crow's and Yvonne Porcella's books in the Bibliography for two artists' exploration of the roots of their designs.

Working with dense stitching is an easier design project because you eliminate color as a decision. In dense stitching you are dealing just with light and dark. First, you find a theme for your work—things that are meaningful to you—and the style you like. For example, see the vest with fans made by Kathy Pierce (Fig. 7-1), who likes the style of Jean Wells (listed in the Bibliography). Kathy has used the fan motif in many creative ways.

When planning your design, you need a cen-

Flower quilt block, one of six designs used to make a dense quilt. Each block is a different appliqué design used in a circle.

Fig. 7-1. *Kathy Pierce's 100-percent cotton vest of her own design of fans, featuring squiggle dense machine stitch. 1989.*

ter of interest, something that attracts the viewer's eye right away. The center of interest may be accented with a different stitch, a bit of sheen, or in pieced work of a contrasting color. The scale of the design also needs to be considered. On dense work, if the design is too small, it does not work. The best balance for the dense quilting is one-half dense stitching and one-half puffed area.

Consider the following ideas to help you get started. I hope your own experiences will add to them.

Do you prefer an asymmetrical or symmetrical arrangement? Let's think of quilts for a moment. Do you feel comfortable with the conventionally placed designs or do you like the quilt designs that flow over the surface in no regular order? I know that a symmetrical design makes me feel more comfortable and puts order in things,

but another side of me says an asymmetrical design is more exciting and more emotional, even though I sometimes feel a certain discontent as I stitch it. I really want to handle curves and free-form compositions. Once, right after making an asymmetrical hanging, I made the very symmetrical piece shown in Fig. 5-13. It was a compulsive act, as if I were afraid the right side of my brain might get the upper hand. See Fig. 7-2, part 1 for examples of asymmetrical and symmetrical arrangements.

Think of your design as having three or more central elements: three, five, seven, etc. Uneven numbers are better design elements than even numbers. Recall the large papa bear, the middle-sized momma bear, and the small baby bear? Does your design have these elements? It may have more to it, but the things that stand out are the

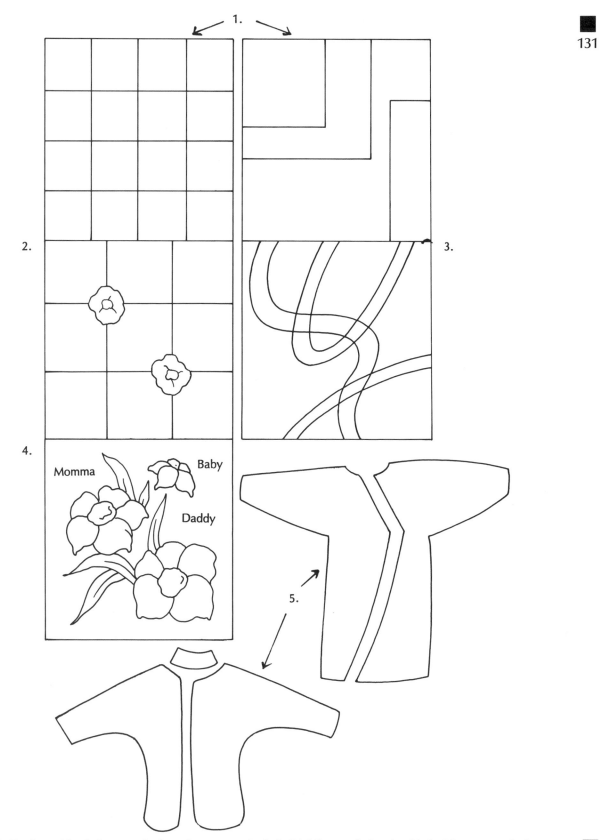

Fig. 7-2. *Design aids. 1. Symmetrical and asymmetrical. 2. Dividing a design in thirds. Place central elements on intersections. 3. Curved lines run to the sides rather than the corners. 4. Three bears. 5. Garment cutouts for designing. Used with permission of* American Quilter *and Lois Ericson.*

OFF ON YOUR OWN

three figures. See if you can find evidence of this theory at the next art show you attend. See Fig. 7-2, part 4.

Another use of the three-design motif is not putting the horizon or center of interest at the halfway mark of the design you are making or the photo you are taking. Divide your picture in thirds both ways. Place the main design elements on the intersections of the grid. Don't put an important object in the middle; put it to one side instead. See Fig. 7-2, part 2.

Lines should not go out of the corners of your design; instead, have them leave at the sides. A line to the corner makes your eye leave the composition. Remember, "A straight line is a line of duty; a curved line is a line of beauty." See Fig. 7-2, part 3.

In *American Quilter* (spring 1989), Lois Ericson shares a good method for beginning the design of a garment. See Fig. 7-2, part 5. Cut these garment shapes from index cards. Lay over photographs in newspapers or magazines until you find an arrangement (usually asymmetrical) that pleases you. Draw the idea you find until you are happy with it. Translate the idea into piecing or dense stitching, and you have your own unique design ready for a garment. Try placing your shapes on the nature drawings and photographs in *Art of the Needle* (listed in the Bibliography).

■ Quilted Jackets for the Larger Figure

When I was selling clothes, many heavier women wanted quilted jackets, and I would custom-make jackets for them. Here are some tips I discovered. Use lighter-weight batting or decorate just the top portion of the garment to shift emphasis toward the face. The green wool cape in the color section is a flattering garment for the heavier woman, for the design features are in the shoulder area and the cape flows over rather than clings to the figure. With age, upper arms tend to get larger and a common alteration is to add gussets under the arm. Using a pattern with a larger arm hole eliminates this alteration.

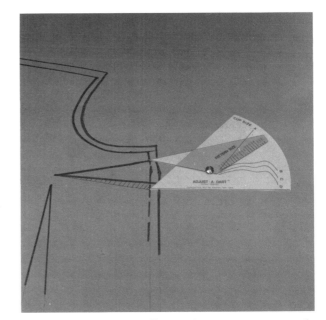

Fig. 7-3. *Adjust-A-Dart™. A nifty notion to correctly place darts in garments.*

By far the most frequent alteration is the addition of a bust dart or positioning a bust dart correctly for the figure. Adjust-A-Dart (see Fig. 7-3) a new notion available from Perfect Notion, helps with marking bust darts correctly. Good directions come with this inexpensive notion.

To take you step by step through the bust dart alteration, I'm indebted to Barbara Weiland and the April 1990 issue of *Sew News*. (Used with slight changes by permission. Copyright © 1990 by PJS Publications, Inc., Peoria, Illinois.) Directions are also in *Mother Pletsch's Painless Sewing* (listed in the Bibliography).

Wearing a properly fitted bra, determine your bust position by measuring from the center of your shoulder to your bust point, then from bust point to bust point. [See Fig. 7-4, part 1.] Measure and mark the intersection of these two measurements on your pattern, remembering to divide the bust-point-to-bust-point measurement in half when measuring from pattern center front. [See Fig. 7-4, part 2.]

From the bust point, draw three lines: Line A at a slightly downward angle to the side seam [this will later form the side dart]; Line B to the

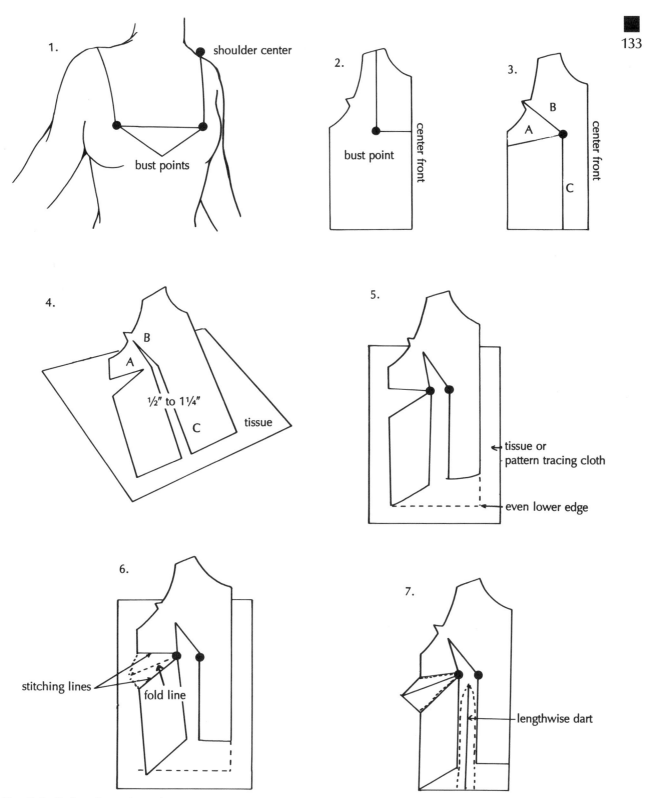

1. shoulder center

bust points

2. bust point

center front

3. A B C

center front

4. B A

½" to 1¼"

C

tissue

5. tissue or pattern tracing cloth

even lower edge

6. stitching lines

fold line

7. lengthwise dart

Fig. 7-4. *Redrawing a bust dart.*

front arm hole notch center; and Line C straight down to the waistline [this will form a waistline dart; see Fig. 7-4, part 3].

In general, Line A should be fairly high under the arm and drop at a slight angle. However, this will vary on individual figures. I suggest testing the pattern with the bustline dart alteration in muslin so you can adjust the dart placement to suit your taste and figure.

Slash the pattern on Line A to but not through the bust point and from the bottom of Line C through the bust point and along Line B, stopping just short of the arm hole edge. Place tissue paper or pattern tracing cloth under the slashed pattern.

Spread the pattern along Line B-C the necessary amount—at Line C, approximately $\frac{1}{2}''$ [1.3cm] for a C cup, $\frac{3}{4}''$ [2cm] for a D cup and 1-$\frac{1}{4}''$ [3cm] or more for larger sizes. As you spread the tissue, a bust dart will open up along Line A. Tape the adjusted pattern to the tissue. [See Fig. 7-4, part 4.]

Even the pattern lower edge on the added tissue [see Fig. 7-4, part 5].

The noted adjustment will create extra bodice length needed to cover a fuller figure.

Draw a dart foldline in the center of the newly formed dart area, stopping 1" [2.5cm] to 2" [5cm] from the bust point.

In general, fuller figures require a shorter line; less-full figures require a longer line. To determine the best foldline length for your figure, test first on muslin.

Draw dart stitching lines from the dart outer edges to the end of the fold. [See Fig. 7-4, part 6.]

Fold out the dart and straighten the side seam. This creates the outer dart point cutting line. Trim away excess adjustment tissue.

To take up the excess fullness created along the pattern lower edge, make a lengthwise dart from that edge to 1" [2.5cm] to [5cm] below the bust [see Fig. 7-4, part 7], determining the exact point on a muslin as noted previously.

In addition, some patterns offer helpful pattern markings and instructions for adding or adjusting darts. Check pattern books for patterns with logos noting such personalized fit features.

Now that you have a pattern for a jacket that is uniquely yours, let's make a densely quilted jacket. Cut outside shell fabric, batting, and backing with the pattern flat, adding $\frac{1}{2}''$ (1.3cm) all around the outside edges. Mark the darts carefully. Plan a design that will not interfere with the darts. The all-over dense machine-quilted design is good. Complete your quilting as directed in Chapter 6, not quilting inside the dart area. Pin darts, shoulder and side seams, and try on for fit. Make any alterations. Cut lining from altered pieces. Now sew the darts in the lining and outside piece. Cut out excess dart fabric and finger press the dart flat. Pin side seam edges of darts open. Finish as directed in Chapter 6.

Books to help with wardrobe planning and clothing construction for the larger woman include *Fashion Design for the Plus Size, Sew Big,* and *Big and Beautiful* (listed in the Bibliography).

■ Half-Hour Vest Lining

If you have completed a beautiful outer shell for a vest and want to line it, try my lining method. It will take approximately one-half hour and is completely machine stitched.

First, check that side seams of the back and sides are the same size. Pin the shoulder and side seams and make any fitting adjustments. Use your outer shell pieces as a pattern to cut the lining.

Pin in place ties or loops for closures.

Sew the shoulder seam of the outer shell and lining separately. Finger-press outer shell seam and pin. Press the lining seam.

On your work surface place lining and outer shell right sides together. Pin. Sew with the wrong side of outer shell up and sew arm hole seams. Sew the bottom back, leaving a 6″ (1.5dm) opening in the middle. Starting at the bottom of the side seam, sew across bottom front, up front, around neckline, down second front, and across bottom front to the second bottom side seam. See

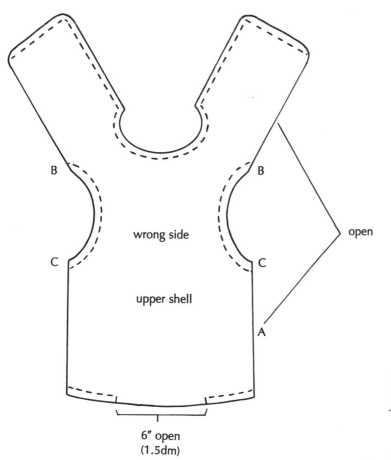

wrong side

upper shell

open

B

B

C

C

A

6″ open
(1.5dm)

Fig. 7-5. *Vest lining. This becomes easy once you practice a bit. I recently have found the same directions in* Mother Pletsch's Painless Sewing *(listed in Bibliography).*

Fig. 7-5. Clip curves. Trim the outer shell seam to $\frac{1}{4}''$ (6mm). Check to be sure side seams match exactly. Adjust.

Reverse by putting your hand in the back side seam A, reaching up, and pulling one front through the hole. With your hand in the *same* side seam hole (A), pull the second front through. Your vest is now right-side-out.

Reach up through the opening left on the bottom back and grab points B and C under one arm. Holding on to points B and C, pull through the opening. Pin seam B/C and bottom back/bottom front seam matching exactly. Pin bottom seam. You have a circle with the outer shell pieces together and the lining together. Sew the circle, which closes the side seams. Pull the seam back in place inside the vest and repeat with the other side. Pin the opening at bottom back.

Finger-press and pin the outside seams so that the lining is on the back and the outer shell is on the front in a sharp seam. Top-stitch using your blind-hem attachment and moving the needle position. It's not vital to top stitch but it does keep the seam in place and reinforces the stitching. The top stitching may interfere somewhat with the design, but I always top stitch. As you top stitch, you sew the bottom back seam in place.

Now wasn't that easy? My friend Glenda George taught me this method, which she learned in a tailoring class in California.

■ Boots

These indoor boots (see Fig. 7-6) make people smile and keep their feet warm at the same time. The directions were originally adapted from Jean Ray Laury's *Quilted Clothing* (listed in the Bibliography). The design is by Margaret Bowman. I sold many and made many to order when I worked craft shows. At indoor craft shows I wore a pair to draw attention to my booth. They make great

Fig. 7-6. *Boots made by Elizabeth Chalk from leftover quilt blocks. Directions for making them are in the text (Chapter 7). 1990.*

presents for your friends and family in cold winter climates. People think they look like mukluks, boots worn by Eskimos, and so they do.

Shopping List

☐ Outer Fabric—½ yd. (.5m) of fabric with some weight. It can be velveteen, corduroy, pieced cotton, cotton/polyester, or upholstery fabric that's not too stiff. You want the fabric to be fun; maybe match it with a robe. It's a good way to use up scraps from the end of a project or some piecing you have saved. Consider adding tassels, cording, ribbons, or any trim you have. If you plan to wash your boots, preshrink all fabrics.

☐ ¼ yd. (.2m) Naugahyde, heavy suede, or leather for soles.

☐ ½ yd. (.5m) cotton fabric for lining.

☐ ½ yd. (.5m) batting. Try the thinner craft batting here. There are places in construction that you must sew on the batting, and this batting is firmer and won't get caught in the presser foot.

☐ Thread to match.

☐ Sewing machine with heavy needle (leather needle if using leather soles).

How to Cut Boot Parts

See Fig. 7-7.

In your bare feet, step on a piece of pattern paper. Draw around your one foot (usually it is not necessary to have both left and right foot). Add ½″ (1.3cm) seam allowance to drawing. This is the pattern for the sole.

To make the sole strip, measure around the line drawn for the foot pattern and add ½″ (1.3cm) seam allowance on the ends. This is the sole strip,

Fig. 7-7. *Boots. 1. Pattern pieces and sample measurements for making your patterns. 2. Sewing the boot uppers to the bottom part is the most complicated procedure in making the boots. 3. Front view of toe piece.*

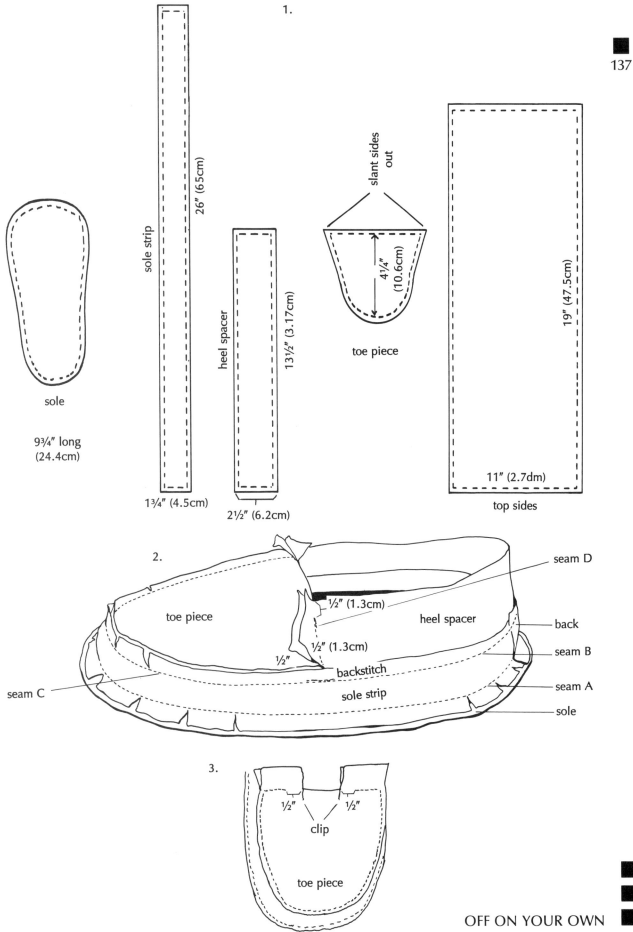

1.

sole strip
26" (65cm)
1¾" (4.5cm)

heel spacer
13½" (3.17cm)
2½" (6.2cm)

slant sides
out
4¼"
(10.6cm)
toe piece

19" (47.5cm)
11" (2.7dm)
top sides

sole
9¾" long
(24.4cm)

2.

seam D

toe piece

½" (1.3cm)

heel spacer

back

½" (1.3cm)

backstitch

seam B

½"

seam A

seam C

sole strip

sole

3.

½"   ½"

clip

toe piece

OFF ON YOUR OWN

and it is $1\text{-}\frac{3}{4}''$ (4.5cm) wide. Measure with a tape measure. I have sometimes made the sole strip from a piece of Naugahyde.

The heel spacer is $2\text{-}\frac{1}{2}''$ (6.2cm) wide sole by one-half the length measurement of the sole plus $\frac{1}{2}''$ (1.3cm) seam allowance. This wraps around the back of the boot above the sole strip and connects to the toe piece. Fold the sole in half and measure on your drawn pattern line. Add seam allowance. See my sample measurements to be sure you are near the correct measurement. See Fig. 7-7, part 1.

The toe piece is cut from the sole and is half the length. Fold the sole in half again for this measurement. Add a $\frac{1}{2}''$ (1.3cm) seam allowance all around the toe piece. Slant sides out on your toe-piece pattern, as in the drawing. This extra amount gives room over the arch of the foot.

The final pieces are the top sides and the height is up to you. Do you want boots up to your knees? Their width is the measurement around the top of the heel piece, across the front of the toe piece. Add $\frac{1}{2}''$ (1.3cm) seam allowance on all sides except the top. This piece and the toe are the pieces to quilt and decorate. Complete the decoration before doing the final cutting.

Cut lining pieces the same dimensions as outer pieces. Double pieces for your two feet.

Cut batting for each of the outer fabric pieces.

Sewing Order

Remember to use $\frac{1}{2}''$ (1.3cm) seam allowances throughout.

Note: You can understand the sewing order clearly if you sew a lining together first. On the lining it is easier to see the seams when there is no batting with which to contend.

Pin batting to each outer fabric piece and machine-quilt. Include batting on the inside of the sole. Quilt with three straight rows.

Sew the back seam of the sole strip, making a circle. Pin the right side of the sole strip to the right side of the sole, placing the back seam of the sole strip at the back of the sole. Sew. Clip the curved areas of the sole spacer.

Note: Actually, I prefer to sew the sole spacer another way. Start with a longer piece. To be sure to have adequate length, start sewing 2" (2.5cm) from the end and sew to within 2" (2.5cm) of the second end. Sew the back seam and complete the open part of the seam. This takes care of any inaccuracies in measuring.

For the heel spacer, find the center and pin to the center back of the sole/sole strip assembly. Sew from the center back seam to within $\frac{1}{2}''$ (1.3cm) of the front of the heel spacer. Backstitch. This leaves the seam allowance of the front of the heel spacer open. Sew from back seam to within $\frac{1}{2}''$ (1.3cm) of the front on the other side. See Fig. 7-7, part 2.

For the toe piece, find the center front of the sole strip and toe piece. Mark. Pin the toe piece to the sole strip, right sides together. Clip into the seam allowance of the toe piece so the toe piece will fit around the sole strip. Sew, leaving $\frac{1}{2}''$ (1.3cm) seam allowance unsewn on top of the toe piece. Backstitch. Sew the seam allowance of the heel spacer to the open seam allowance of the toe piece. Leave $\frac{1}{2}''$ (1.3cm) seam allowance of the top unsewn. Backstitch. Clip $\frac{1}{2}''$ (1.3cm) seam allowance on top of the toe piece.

Seam the back seam of the top sides. See the previous note. You may want to shape this seam some if your legs are thin. The boot, however, is meant to be soft and not very tight fitting. Pin the right sides of the upper piece to the bottom boot assembly with the upper-piece seam in the center back. Sew. The clips in the toe piece enable you to get around this seam. You may find it necessary to clip the top toe piece more than twice.

Sew linings in the same order.

Insert lining into boots wrong sides together. Cut a 2" (5cm) wide strip of one of your fabrics to finish top and connect the lining and outer boot. Sew with right sides together, lapping the end of the seam. Turn under edge of strip and hand-stitch to inside. Add any further decorations.

I will sometimes add batting to lining pieces

of the sole and sole spacer and quilt in a grid. This gives extra warmth and a nice feel of quilted fabric on the bare foot.

It's a good idea to make templates of two or three sizes so you are always prepared to cut and sew a pair of boots.

If you are interested in making more outdoor shoes and slippers order: "Pitter-Patters," Artful Illusions, P.O. Box 278, Ector, TX 75439-0278. Send $1.50 for their catalog of patterns.

■ Skirts

The first skirt has dense stitching at the bottom. See Fig. 7-8 of a white skirt with pearl buttons.

Choose a pattern that is straight or relatively straight at the bottom. The pattern I used has four gores that are not overly flared.

Construct the entire skirt except for the hem. If you are using cotton, you may want to line the skirt. Construct the lining and attach it when sewing the waist band. The lining helps cover the dense stitching on the inside. I use the serger or French seams for the side seams.

Mark with a washable pencil where the hem is to be. This is easiest to do on the ironing board. Draw your design on the skirt bottom.

Still working on the ironing board, turn the skirt to the wrong side. Add batting to the back of the skirt design area from the hemline to the top of the design. Add a backing fabric behind the batting. Pin. It is necessary to piece batting

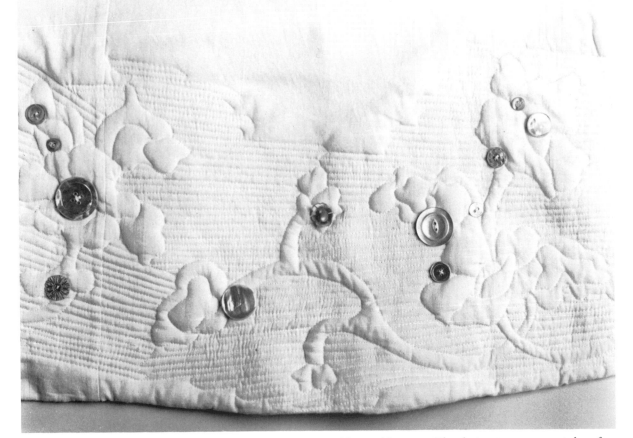

Fig. 7-8. *Detail of lined white skirt of 100-percent cotton with pearl buttons. The design pattern was taken from an appliqué design in Jean Rae Laury's* Quilted Clothing *(listed in the Bibliography). Batting is in the design area only. 1985.*

and backing to form curves at the skirt bottom. The resulting skirt will stand out some. To balance the weight, repeat the design all around the bottom.

"Set" your design and stitch the background. When completed, trim out excess batting and backing at the top of the design. Leave batting and backing in the hem to prevent a see-through area between the hem and design when you wear the skirt in the light.

Another option for the dense skirt is to design an area for the left front of the skirt from waist to hem. This option can be very flattering. You can use a front-wrap pattern and place the design on the front of the flap. See Fig. 7-9.

Another skirt you may want to try was made by my daughter, Elizabeth Chalk (see the color section). This skirt (Fig. 7-10) has an enlarged Seminole band for decoration, but other designs can be used. The skirt has a flexible waistband

Fig. 7-9. *Wrap skirt with dense machine stitching on the flap. 1984. Owner: Peggy Krieg.*

CREATING YOUR OWN DESIGNS

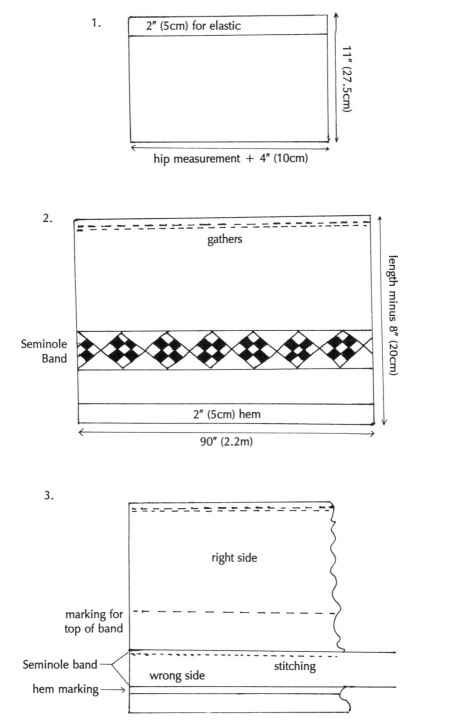

Fig. 7-10. *Seminole band skirt construction. 1. Cut top panel. 2. Cut bottom skirt panel. 3. Place design band on bottom skirt panel.*

and eliminates extra fabric in the waist. This design is slimming.

Cut a top skirt panel 11″ (2.7dm) deep by your hip measurement plus 4″ (1dm) for the width. Seam sides on the serger or make French seams. See Fig. 7-10.

Cut the bottom panel the length you desire, adding a 2″ (5cm) hem and subtracting 8″ (2dm) for the top section. The width of the bottom panel is 90″ (2.5m) or two widths of fabric. Sew *one* side seam.

Construct your Seminole band. See the section on quilt blocks in Chapter 5 for making the enlarged Seminole block.

Mark the hemline. Mark placement of the bottom of the design band. Sew the design band to the marking, with the right side of the design band to the right side of skirt. Press design band up. Press under top seam allowance on the design band. Pin to the skirt. Be careful not to stretch the bias of the triangles of your band. Does the design band match at the opened side of the skirt? If not, add more fabric to the skirt width or cut some off. After you have made adjustments, top-stitch the bottom and the top of the design band. Top-stitching the top of the design band attaches the band to the skirt. Top-stitching the bottom of the design band just balances the stitching.

Pin second side seam, carefully matching your design, and sew.

Gather the top of the skirt bottom panel and attach to the bottom of the top panel. Serge seam to finish. For easier gathering, zigzag over a heavy cord, such as a buttonhole twist or string, not catching the cord with stitches. Draw up gathers as usual, stitch, and remove cord when seam is finished.

Blind-stitch the hem. Lap 2″ (5cm) of skirt top to the underside and blind-stitch, leaving an opening for elastic. Measure the waist for elastic. Insert elastic in the opening using a bodkin or safety pin. Bring elastic ends out and overlap ends. Stitch securely. Pull elastic to the inside and sew the opening closed.

Your new skirt is ready to wear. I like to wear this skirt rather long. It feels good and, if made from cotton, is cooler than pants in summer.

■ Machine-Quilted Quilts

How can you transfer what you have learned about machine-quilting jackets to machine-quilting whole quilts? All the rules are the same (see Chapter 3). You are just handling much more fabric. Provide for the additional fabric by giving yourself more space to hold the fabric at the left and back of your machine. You roll the sides of the quilt and pin them to control the bulk going through the machine. Leave open the area on which you currently are working.

Use nickel-plated safety pins instead of straight pins to put your sandwich together, because the regular pins come out—I learned this the hard way. You still stitch by starting at one side and working to the other side. The best help I have found is in Harriet Hargrave's *Heirloom Machine Quilting* (listed in the Bibliography).

On my first try, I machine-quilted a scrap quilt made of 3″ (7.5cm) squares. The feed dogs were up. I quilted a straight line through the center of each square. I used the even-feed foot and started in the middle of one quilt side. See Fig. 7-11. Then I stitched new rows on either side of the center row. After doing all the rows on one side, I turned the quilt *90 degrees* and repeated on the other side. It was an easy first project and it looked good.

The second quilt is called Migrating Geese, a quick quilt that again used scraps. I quilted it using the Barbara Johannah method (listed in the Bibliography) with the feed dogs down and the darning foot on the machine. It was harder to get good free swings with the quilt bulk to handle at the same time. See Fig. 7-12. Migrating Geese is a pattern by bjs designs, © 1987, by Brenda Schmidt, Box 252, Stratham, NH 03885.

The third quilt is shown in the color section. The strata were made quickly on the serger, but I found I could not put the blocks together accurately with the serger, so I switched to the regular machine. I quilted the quilt with a combination of feed dogs up, Barbara Johannah method

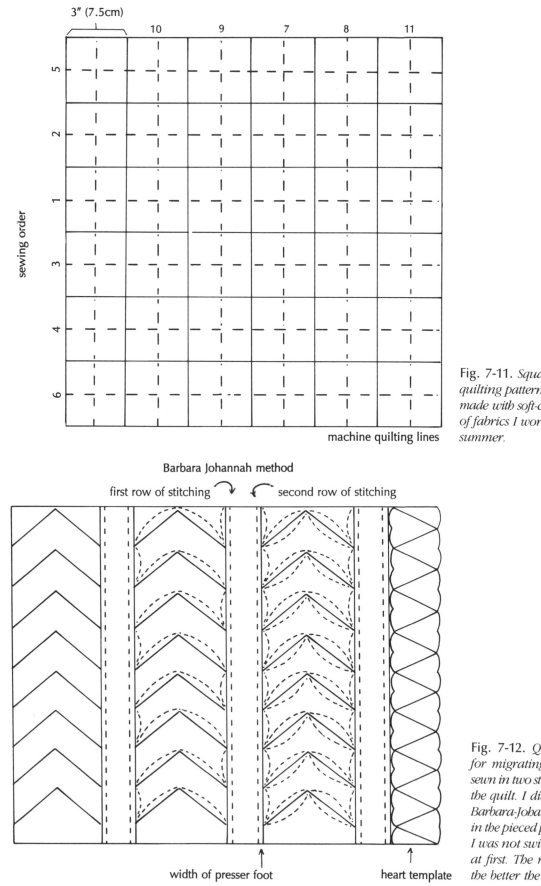

3″ (7.5cm)

10 9 7 8 11

sewing order

5

2

1

3

4

6

machine quilting lines

Fig. 7-11. *Square quilt and quilting pattern. This quilt is made with soft-colored scraps of fabrics I worked with one summer.*

Barbara Johannah method

first row of stitching ↷ ↶ second row of stitching

width of presser foot

heart template

Fig. 7-12. *Quilting pattern for migrating geese design, sewn in two stitchings through the quilt. I did not mark the Barbara-Johannah-style rows in the pieced part of the quilt. I was not swinging very well at first. The more I relaxed, the better the work became.*

OFF ON YOUR OWN ■

Fig. 7-13. *Dense machine-quilted white quilt made of 100-percent cotton. The circular flower forms design was taken from quilt appliqué patterns. I drew one-quarter of the design on paper and then set up a homemade light table to draw the complete design. 1986.*

on colored blocks, and feed dogs down on designs in the white blocks. By this time I was feeling more comfortable handling the bulk. I'm eager to try again with my annual scrap quilt.

Using the dense machine quilting in a quilt presents a different problem. Since the back is so messy, it has to be covered. See Fig. 7-13.

How to Cover the Back of the Quilt

Sew the horizontal rows of blocks of your quilt together. See Fig. 7-14. Measure a strip of sewn horizontal blocks. Cut as many lining pieces as you have rows.

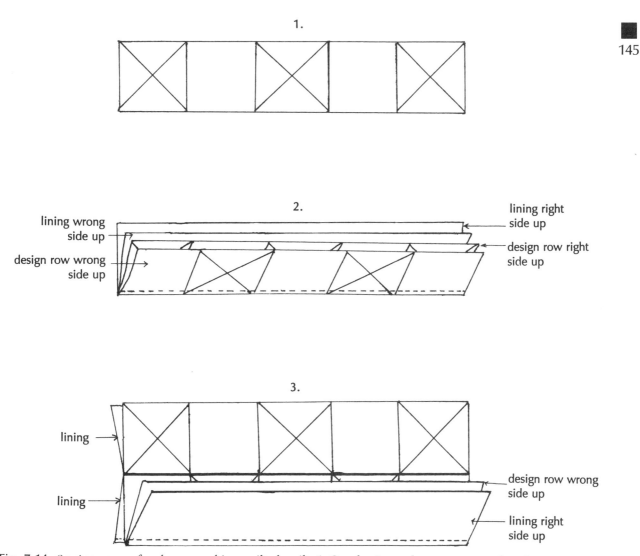

1.

2.

lining wrong side up

design row wrong side up

lining right side up

design row right side up

3.

lining

lining

design row wrong side up

lining right side up

Fig. 7-14. *Sewing rows of a dense machine-quilted quilt. 1. One horizontal row sewn together. Sew remaining horizontal rows. 2. First row of stitching through four layers. 3. Second row of stitching. Be sure to pin and match the corners of your blocks. Seam allowance ¼" (6mm) throughout. Not drawn to scale to allow for better viewing.*

Place one lining strip right-side-up on your table. Place the second lining strip right-side-down on top of the first. Place one horizontal quilted strip right-side-up on the linings. Place a second quilted horizontal strip right-side-down on your pile. If this sounds confusing, check it out with four marked pieces of paper. Sew and match all intersections of horizontal rows.

Open up and spread the first lining strip over the top horizontal row and the second lining strip over the second horizontal row. Pin.

On top of the second horizontal row, place another horizontal quilted strip wrong-side-down. Under the other three pieces place another lining strip right-side-up. Pin. Sew. Open up and smooth everything in place. Pin.

Continue in this manner until all rows are added. Bind as usual.

In some areas of your design, it may be appropriate to tie French knots or add buttons to further finish the layers. The hanging shown in Fig. 5-13 has only one lining, which is attached

OFF ON YOUR OWN

as I describe. If your blocks are large, you may want to sew the lining to the horizontal rows as described above; then each block will have a separate lining.

▪ Doodles

If you have just finished a pieced project and have wonderful bits and pieces of fabric left over, you may be wondering what to do with them. You can make a "doodle" cloth that might well turn out to be your finest creation. Start with smaller pieces and add increasingly larger ones at the straight edges. I usually go around the edges in log-cabin style, but no areas are regular. One of the rules that I sometimes break is not to get into new fabric to finish the doodle. Don't plan; just sew. "Marvin's Piano" (Fig. 7-15) is a doodle quilt project. It is finished by sewing and flipping black fabric to square the piece. I then added batting and a backing, machine-quilted, and then bound the piece. "Kite" (Fig. 7-16) is another doodle cloth. Look at the lines in both photographs and see if you can tell where I sewed first. I usually look forward to finishing a garment just so I can play with the scraps.

Fig. 7-15. *Doodle cloth entitled "Marvin's Piano." 1983.*

is a trick, because people who actually buy one-of-a-kind wearables account for only ten percent of the population. I was most successful in the Washington, D.C., and Richmond, Virginia, areas, which were within comfortable travel distances for me. Some of my regular customers designed ideas they wanted me to sew. That was a great experience.

To better understand how to operate a small business, I took a course at a local technical school that proved to be very informative. There I learned how to get proper licenses, pay my taxes, keep records, create care tags, order forms, have business cards made, and everything else needed to run my business. The photography and setup equipment necessary to work a craft or art show take time and money to produce. *Crafts Report* (listed in the Bibliography) is valuable in helping locate shows, trends, and many of the how-to's. I hired assistants one at a time for three afternoons per week. At the same time I was selling at craft shows; teaching; and selling notions, books, and unusual fabrics. Yet even with all of this activity, I did not earn my living; I only kept my "hobby" from eating into the family budget.

I learned that three things were necessary to make a living, and I was not willing to do them. First, I needed to push myself and my products harder by entering more shows and competitions. Second, I needed to produce more, which would have meant hiring more help and becoming a supervisor instead of a creator. Third, I needed to standardize the product so that I could produce more *faster*. But I wanted to keep designing new things, not continually work on old ideas. As it was, I would come home from a show and make many of the same designs in different sizes or colors, because individuals had requested more of what they saw at my display.

With smaller quilted items such as totes, pillows, and especially place mats, you do not make enough money for your effort. I kept records of the time spent on each garment, gave myself a dollar-per-hour figure plus expenses, and doubled it to get the price. If I knew the market wouldn't bear the price, I lowered it. I also learned never to take a special order, even from your best friend, without one-half of the price as a deposit.

Fig. 7-16. *Doodle cloth entitled "Kite."*

■ Selling Your Quilted Clothing

The day will come when your production has increased, your relatives all have your wonderful creations, and you need more fabric. You decide to sell your creations. I did just that twelve years ago, selling at craft shows and through specialty shops on consignment for the next eight years. What did I learn from the experience that might help you?

The contact I had with the public was very enjoyable, although it was scary at first. I met many wonderful people and received constructive feedback on my work. The feedback was not all positive, and my ego had to take some bumps, but my work improved. Finding the right market niche

Never present anything at a show you are not willing to make again. My example of this is frog closures. I made my own, showed jackets with them attached, and the customer then wanted frogs on her jacket. But I hated to make frogs, so I soon learned to show nothing with frogs!

Consignment never worked well for me. Clothes need to be tried on and worn around to show best. It takes special store management to show your work well.

To be successful you need lots of energy and you need to be willing to work hard. Shows usually are three-day affairs. You go to the area, find a motel, head to the site, unpack and set up, act friendly to total strangers for three days, pack up, and drive home to start sewing again.

In all my experiences with craft shows, the satisfactions have outweighed any negatives. I met interesting people, got new ideas, saw new places, and was able to afford more fabric. If you decide to try it, I wish you success.

■ Afterword

We have come a long way together. How are your projects progressing? If you wish, write to me at the following address with your problems as well as your new discoveries, so I can help you and celebrate with you. The "Kite" doodle was made during one of my recent moves and symbolizes our new creative wings.

My address is
Nancy Lobmiller Moore
P.O. Box 496
Wake Forest, NC 27488-0496

Bibliography

The following books are my favorites. I buy and read many sewing and quilting books and magazines, always looking for a new way or new idea.

■ Books

Avery, Virginia. *Quilts to Wear*. New York: Charles Scribner's Sons, 1982. Lots of originality, but directions are not detailed.

Beaney, Jan. *The Art of the Needle*. New York: Pantheon Books, 1988. An inspiring book with a good section on design and wonderful examples.

Bennett, D.J. *Machine Embroidery with Style*. Seattle: Madrona Publishers, Inc., 1980.

Bishop, Edna B., and Marjorie Arch. *Super Sewing*. Philadelphia: J.B. Lippincott, 1962.

Bonesteel, Georgia. *Lap Quilting with Georgia Bonesteel*. Birmingham, Alabama: Oxmoor House, Inc., 1982.

Boriss, Barbara Bell. *The Original Log Cabin and Vest Book*. Westminster, California: Yours Truly Publications, 1983. Directions are adequate. Log cabins are made by the long method. She machine-quilts backs and hand-stitches fronts. There is no emphasis on creativity. The finishing method is similar to mine, and I like her mitering of double French bias.

Bradkin, C.G. *The Seminole Patchwork Book*. Westminster, California: Yours Truly Publications, 1980. No longer in print. Nice pictures of work, easy-to-follow drawings, some measurement mistakes. Note: Yours Truly Publications is no longer in business. You may find some of their books in stores with back stock or used book stores.

Brown, Gail. *Sensational Silk*. Portland, Oregon: Palmer/Pletsch Associates, 1982.

Brown, Gail, and Tammy Young. *Innovative Serging*. Radnor, Pennsylvania: Chilton Book Company, 1989. The very latest on the serger. Contains clothing construction techniques with wovens as well as knits.

Crow, Nancy. *Nancy Crow Quilts and Influences*. Paducah, Kentucky: American Quilter's Society, 1990. Beautiful book on roots of Nancy's designs. Wonderful colors and wonderful piecing. The address for ordering is American Quilters Society, P.O. Box 3290, Paducah, KY 42002-3290.

Dittman, Margaret. *The Fabric Lover's Scrapbook*. Radnor, Pennsylvania: Chilton Book Company, 1988. Lots of neat techniques, well explained.

Dodson, Jackie. *Know Your Bernina,* 2d ed. Radnor, Pennsylvania: Chilton Book Company, 1988. There is a similar manual specific to each major sewing machine. This is another book to keep by the machine and try the ideas.

Edwards, Betty. *Drawing on the Right Side of the Brain*. Boston: Houghton Mifflin Co., 1979.

Ericson, Lois, and Diane Frode. *Sewing It Yourself*. Self-published, 1981.

Ericson, Lois, and Diane Frode. *Design It Yourself*. Self-published, 1980.

Ericson, Lois. *Texture—A Closer Look*. Self-published, 1987.

Ericson, Lois. *Pleats*. Self-published, 1989.

Ericson, Lois. *Tucks*. Self-published, 1988. The address for the Ericson books is P.O. Box 5222, Salem, OR 97304.

Fanning, Robbie and Tony. *Complete Book of Machine Quilting*. Radnor, Pennsylvania: Chilton Book Company, 1980.

Fanning, Robbie, and Tony. *Complete Book of Machine Embroidery*. Radnor, Pennsylvania: Chilton Book Company, 1986. The *Complete Book of Machine Embroidery* and *Machine Quilting* are complete on their subjects, and are musts if you love your machine. They both take study and practice. Set up your machine and try the ideas. They contain freeing the machine but not dense quilting.

Fons, Marianne, and Elizabeth Porter. *Classic Quilted Vest*. Westminster, California: Yours Truly Publications, 1982. Directions are good. The emphasis is on handwork. The designs now are outdated.

Hallock, Anita. *Fast Patch*. Radnor, Pennsylvania: Chilton Book Company, 1989. A neat new way to make quilt blocks swiftly, it takes some study.

Hargrave, Harriet. *Heirloom Machine Quilting*. Westminster, California: Yours Truly Publications/Dale Burdett, 1987. Shows some dense quilting on clothing in a more controlled form. Emphasis is in book on quilts, not clothing. The book is out of print, but a new edition is available from C&T. Address for C&T is 5021 Blum Rd., Martinez, CA 94553.

Haywood, Dixie. *Crazy Quilting with a Difference*. Bethany, Oklahoma: Sissortail Publications, 1981. The address for ordering is Sissortail Publications, P.O. Box 735, Bethany, OK 73008.

Horton, Roberta. *An Amish Adventure*. Martinez, California: C&T Publishing, 1983. The address for ordering is C&T Publications, 5021 Blum Rd., Martinez, CA 94553.

Johannah, Barbara. *Half Square Triangles—Exploring Design*. Self-published, 1987.

Johannah, Barbara. *Quick Quiltmaking Handbook*. Self-published, 1979.

Johannah, Barbara. *Continuous Curve Quilting*. Self-published, 1980. Anyone who wants to save time and find clever ways to do sewing-machine piecing and machine quilting needs Johannah's three books. Barbara is the originator of many new ideas. The address to order books is P.O. Box 396, Navarro, CA 95463.

Ladbury, Ann. *Quick Casual Clothes*. New York: Doubleday and Company, Inc., 1985.

Laury, Jean Ray. *Quilted Clothing*. Birmingham, Alabama: Oxmoor House, 1982. Lots of ideas.

Directions assume you know a lot about sewing.

Mashuta, Mary. *Wearable Art for Real People.* Martinez, California: C&T Publishing, 1989. The address for ordering is C&T Publishing, 5021 Blum Rd., Martinez, CA 94553.

McKelvey, Susan R. *Color for Quilters.* Westminster, California: Yours Truly Publications, 1984. The McKelvey book and Roberta Horton's *Amish Adventure* are wonderful for color choices. They provide nice exercises to work out with a group of friends.

Meilach, Dona Z., and Dee Menagh. *Exotic Needlework.* New York: Crown Publishers, Inc., 1978. Early favorite; well studied. Here again, ethnics are not popular today, but that can change.

Olds, Ruthanne. *Big and Beautiful.* Washington: Acropolis Books, Ltd., 1982.

Palmer, Pati, and Susan Pletsch. *Mother Pletsch's Painless Sewing,* rev. ed. Portland, Oregon: Palmer/Pletsch Associates, 1986. Inexpensive beginning sewing book.

Porcella, Yvonne. *Pieced Clothing.* Self-published, 1980.

Porcella, Yvonne. *Pieced Clothing Variations.* Self-published, 1981. Yvonne is the best piecer. Her books contain easy-to-use ethnic patterns. I'm finding my students and customers prefer commercial patterns, however. Quilting the sleeve areas makes the garment too bulky (true with the Folkwear Pattern as well). I use them but find wider acceptance for commercial patterns.

Porcella, Yvonne. *Yvonne Porcella: A Colorful Book.* Self-published, 1987. Her latest book, this is a beautiful record of her accomplishments. The address for ordering is Porcella Studios, 3619 Shoemake Ave., Modesto, CA 95351.

Poster, Donna. *Speed-Cut Quilts.* Radnor, Pennsylvania: Chilton Book Company, 1989.

Puckett, Marjorie. *String Quilts 'n Things.* Orange, California: Orange Patchwork Publishers, 1979. This book must have come at the right time for me and appealed to my Great Depression

saving values. It remains a favorite. I use muslin where Marjorie uses paper for backing as I am not going to hand-quilt and I dislike removing the paper. The address for ordering is P.O. Box 2557, Orange, CA 92669.

Rose, Helen Whitson. *Quick-and-Easy Strip Quilting.* Mineola, New York: Dover Publications, Inc., 1989. The source of a quick quilt block cutting method.

Rush, Beverly, with Lassie Wittman. *The Complete Book of Seminole Patchwork.* Seattle: Madrona Publishers, Inc., 1982. No longer in print. A very creative book with good history and examples of Seminole Indian work.

Saunders, Jan. *A Step-by-Step Guide to Your Sewing Machine.* Radnor, Pennsylvania: Chilton Book Company, 1990.

Saunders, Jan. *Sew, Serge, Press: Speed Tailoring in the Ultimate Sewing Center.* Radnor, Pennsylvania: Chilton Book Company, 1989.

Saunders, Jan. *Teach Yourself to Sew Better: A Step-by-Step Guide to Your Sewing Machine.* Radnor, Pennsylvania: Chilton Book Company, 1990. A good basic sewing book.

Shaeffer, Claire. *Claire Shaeffer's Fabric Sewing Guide.* Radnor, Pennsylvania: Chilton Book Company, 1989. An encyclopedia of fabrics and how to work with each. A must in a sewer's library.

Schaeffer, Claire. *Claire Schaeffer's Sewing S.O.S.* Radnor, Pennsylvania: Chilton Book Company, 1988. The answer to every sewing problem.

Singer Reference Library. *Decorative Machine Stitching.* Minnetonka, Minnesota: Cy DeCosse, Inc., 1990.

Singer Reference Library. *Quilting by Machine.* Minnetonka, Minnesota: Cy DeCosse, Inc., 1990. Both Singer Reference Library books have lovely color and good examples that are very well done.

Singer Sewing Machine Company. *Singer Instructions for Art Embroidery and Lace Work.* Menlo Park, California: Open Chain Publishing (P.O. Box 2634, Menlo Park, CA 94026), 1990. Full-color reprint of the 1941 edition. It contains all the techniques we are "rediscovering" today, except that the work presented here was sewn without a zigzag machine. It is an impressive book.

Spike, Kathleen. *Sew to Success.* Portland, Oregon: Palmer/Pletsch Associates, 1990.

Stothers, Marilyn. *Curved Strip-Piecing: A New Technique.* Winnipeg, Manitoba, Canada: PH Press, 1988. This book presents a new technique to solve the old problem of piecing curves efficiently. There are other books out there on the subject, but this is uniquely new. The address for ordering is PH Press, 630 Cloutier Dr., Winnipeg, Manitoba, Canada, R3V 1L2.

Thelen, Marilyn. *Sew Big.* Portland, Oregon: Palmer/Pletsch Associates, 1980. If you ever get a chance to attend a Palmer/Pletsch seminar, do so. They are full of new ideas.

Tice, Bill. *Enticements.* New York: Macmillan Publishing Company, 1985.

Vogue Sewing. Butterick Fashion Marketing Co., 1982.

Weiland, Barbara and Leslie Wood. *Clothes Sense.* Portland, Oregon: Palmer/Pletsch Associates, 1984.

Wells, Jean. *Fans.* Martinez, California: C&T Publishing, 1987. Excellent discussion of designing process. The address for ordering is C&T Publishing, 5021 Blum Rd., Martinez, CA 94553.

Wells, Jean. *A Patchworthy Apparel Book.* Westminster, California: Yours Truly Publications, 1981.

Wiechec, Philomena. *Celtic Quilt Designs.* Saratoga, California: Walter and Philomena Wiechec Publishers, 1980. The address for ordering is Celtic Design Co., 19170 Portos Dr., Saratoga, CA 95070.

Zangrillo, Frances Leto. *Fashion Design for the Plus Size.* New York: Fairchild Books and Visuals, 1989.

Zieman, Nancy, with Robbie Fanning. *The Busy Woman's Sewing Book.* Menlo Park, California: Open Chain Publishing, 1989. The address for ordering is P.O. Box 2634, Menlo Park, CA 94026.

■ Magazines

American Quilter, P.O. Box 3290, Paducah, KY 42002-3290. A quilting magazine and association that publishes and sells books. They also sell quilts on consignment.

Crafts Report, P.O. Box 1992, Wilmington, DE 19899. Good help if you want to sell your work. Covers all aspects of business.

Dover Publications, 31 East 2nd St., Mineola, NY 11501. Inexpensive, wonderful design books. Send for needlework catalog.

Fiberarts, 50 College St., Asheville, NC 28801. Latest fiber shows and innovative works. Good for design ideas.

Quilter's Newsletter Magazine, P.O. Box 394, Wheatridge, CO 80033-0394. How-to magazine for quilting by hand and machine.

Sew News, PJS Publications, P.O. Box 1790, Peoria, IL 61656. *Sew News* features sewing techniques and latest fashions, plus sewing machine and serger information.

Threads, Taunton Press, 63 S. Main St., P.O. Box 9976, Newtown, CT 06470-9976. This is a beautifully presented magazine with articles on sewing, knitting, and anything to do with a needle and thread.

Treadleart, 25834-1 Narbonne Ave., Lomita, CA 90717. *Treadleart* is a magazine of machine arts, with all the latest methods for sewing machines. They have a notion and book catalog as well.

The Sewing Update, 2269 Chestnut, Suite 269, San Francisco, CA 94123.

The Serger Update is from the same address as *The Sewing Update.* They both feature timely tips for machinists.

■ ■ ■
Supply List

■ Sources of Fabric

I have dealt with each of these companies and found them reasonable and prompt, with good-quality fabric. You receive monthly samples with your membership charge.

Cabin Fever Calicoes, P.O. Box 550106, Atlanta, GA 30355. Phone: 1-800-762-2246. Cotton fabrics, quilting notions and books are featured.

Fabrics in Vogue, 200 Park Ave., Suite 303 East, New York, NY 10166. Membership charge.

G Street Fabrics, 11854 Rockville Pike, Rockville, MD 20852. Phone: (301) 231-8998. Send for samples of the type of fabric you want. Charge for samples. If you know what you want, call for prompt delivery.

Keepsake Quilting, P.O. Box 1459, Meredith, NH 03253. Phone: (603) 279-3351. They carry cotton fabrics, quilting notions, and books.

Natural Fiber Fabric Club, 521 Fifth Ave., New York, NY 10175. Membership charge.

Seventh Avenue Designer Fabric Club, 701 7th Ave., Suite 900, New York, NY 10036. Membership charge.

Sew Biz, 92 and 94 Harvey St., Radford, VA 24141. Phone: (703) 639-1138. Marianne Beeson, owner. The staff of Sew Biz will assist you in selecting fabrics, buttons, trims, special notions, and tools for your projects. Unusual and hard-to-find items include handmade buttons, tailoring supplies, beads, specialty threads, and cords. Darning feet can be ordered through Sew Biz.

Sew Natural, Route 1, Box 635, Middlesex, NC 27557. They have a wide selection of the hard-to-find cotton knits. Charge for samples.

■ ■ Just Notions

Clotilde, 1909 S.W. First Ave., Fort Lauderdale, FL 33315-2100. Phone: (305) 761-8655 for credit card orders.

Crabtree Sew and Vac, 4325 Glenwood Ave., Raleigh, NC 27612. Phone: (919) 787-6121. Scott Harbour can supply a darning (embroidery) foot for almost any machine. Tell him the brand of machine and whether it is a short, slanted, or long-shank machine.

Nancy's Notions, 333 Beichl Ave., P.O. Box 683, Beaver Dam, WI 53916. Phone: 1-800-765-0690.

The Perfect Notion, 566 Hoyt St., Darien, CT 06820. Catalog is $1.00.

■ Fabric Dyes

Brooks & Flynn, P.O. Box 2639, Rohnert Park, CA 94927-2639. Phone: 1-800-822-2372 for a catalog.

Earth Guild, One Tingle Alley, Asheville, NC 28801. Phone: 1-800-327-8448. They carry other craft supplies as well.

Pro Chemical and Dye, P.O. Box 14, Somerset, MA 02726. Phone: (508) 676-3838. Free catalog.

Index

INDEX

INDEX